If you'd like to contact the authors by e-mail:

Ellen Banks Elwell: ellenelwell@yahoo.com

Joan Bartel Stough: jjstough@msn.com

WHEN THERE'S

Not enough
of Me to Go Around

Life Solutions to
Perfectionism,
People-Pleasing
& Performance Pressures

ELLEN BANKS
ELWELL

JOAN BARTEL
STOUGH

InterVarsity Press
Downers Grove, Illinois

InterVarsity Press
P.O. Box 1400, Downers Grove, IL 60515-1426
World Wide Web: www.ivpress.com
E-mail: mail@ivpress.com

InterVarsity Press® is the book-publishing division of InterVarsity Christian Fellowship/USA®, a student movement active on campus at hundreds of universities, colleges and schools of nursing in the United States of America, and a member movement of the International Fellowship of Evangelical Students. For information about local and regional activities, write Public Relations Dept., InterVarsity Christian Fellowship/USA, 6400 Schroeder Rd., P.O. Box 7895, Madison, WI 53707-7895, or visit the IVCF website at <www.ivcf.org>.

All Scripture quotations, unless otherwise indicated, are taken from the Holy Bible, New International Version®. NIV®. *Copyright ©1973, 1978, 1984 by International Bible Society. Used by permission of Zondervan Publishing House. All rights reserved.*

The stories in this book are based on the lives of real people. In many of these instances names and circumstances have been altered to protect confidentiality of the individuals involved.

Cover illustration: Design Concepts

ISBN 0-8308-2348-4

Printed in the United States of America ∞

Library of Congress Cataloging-in-Publication Data

Elwell, Ellen Banks, 1952-
    When there's not enough of me to go around/Ellen Banks Elwell, Joan
Bartel Stough.
        p. cm.
Includes bibliographical references (p.   )
    ISBN 0-8308-2348-4
    1. Christian women—Religious life. 2. Time management—Religious
aspects—Christianity. I. Stough, Joan Bartel, 1935- II. Title.
    BV4527 .E48 2002
248.8'43—dc21

                                                                2002004055

| P | 16 | 15 | 14 | 13 | 12 | 11 | 10 | 9 | 8 | 7 | 6 | 5 | 4 | 3 | 2 | 1 |
| Y | 15 | 14 | 13 | 12 | 11 | 10 | 09 | 08 | 07 | 06 | 05 | 04 | 03 | 02 |

For
Ellen's mom and sisters:
Betty, Gail and Barbara;
and
Joan's daughters:
Jan, Jeanne and Jill—
special women in our lives who have
given freely of themselves

CONTENTS

Acknowledgments

Special thanks to Amy Cox, Denise Gill, Ruthie Howard, Joan Johnson, Betty Knoedler, Barbara Korell, Nancy Lewis, Shirley Mathews, Carol Ohman, Gail Pflederer and Carla Stough for reading parts of the manuscript for us.

Preface

"There's not enough of me to go around!" We hear the lament—frequently—from women in all walks of life. While this book was still in the idea phase, we shared the concept with our friends, and their common response was "How fast can you get that book written? I need it now!" This book almost didn't get written, though. There were times when we wondered if there was enough of *us* to go around—like the day the computer crashed and we lost the first four chapters.

This book evolved from our own daily dilemmas of balancing families, friends, vocations, church involvement and community service in the context of our love for God and our desire to live purposeful lives. We began by reading, praying, thinking, talking, listening and, finally, writing. We often met for breakfast or lunch at Cantigny Golf Course or Oakfield Restaurant, where empty sugar packets became bookmarks and waiters and waitresses graciously accommodated the papers and books scattered over the table. We wonder how many cups of coffee we consumed!

Perhaps you'll read this book alone. Or maybe you'll read it with a group of women, using the discussion questions at the end of each chapter. However you choose to read it, you'll be encouraged to

☐ accept the fact that you can't be or do it all (and that you can't do life alone)

☐ become intentional about evaluating what's most important

☐ confidently set limits in the context of a purposeful life

We hope that your perspective on life will be renewed, inspiring you to invest your time and energy in things that matter most.

When the pressures and demands of life overwhelm us and we begin to feel trapped, we need more than tips on time management. We need to step back and take a good look at the big picture of life. Can we balance the ever-increasing demands with our desire to be more effective Christian women? Yes! Realizing that God has his special purpose for each of our lives gives us confidence to weigh our choices thoughtfully and intentionally.

When the obvious needs of five thousand hungry people pressed in on Jesus' disciples, the disciples felt trapped and overwhelmed. A little boy in the midst of the crowd became an example for us all. Just as the lad brought his loaves and fishes to Jesus and discovered that Jesus provided more than enough to go around, we can bring our lives to him and receive his provision. We invite you to join us in discovering how to live our lives when it feels like there isn't enough of us to go around!

1

Why Does It Seem Like There's Not Enough of Me to Go Around?

If we live with the feeling that everything
depends on us, that if we don't do everything
it won't get done . . . we will be defeated
by life's pressure.

LLOYD JOHN OGILVIE

*O*ur great-grandmothers would gasp in astonishment if they could see all the labor-saving devices we use today. Long ago, modern appliances were welcomed with gratitude, yet today we feel like engineering failures if we can't program the VCR or dispatch e-mail around the globe daily. Shouldn't our many conveniences simplify our lives? After all, we're not washing clothes by hand or raising chickens. Most of us don't make bread from scratch, although the aroma of freshly baked bread occasionally wafts through our kitchens because of that wonderful invention called the bread machine. When was the last time you spent your summer canning and freezing produce? If we forget to plan dinner or defrost meat in the morning, it's not a problem; we can pop a chicken pot pie into the microwave right before dinner.

Why then do we come to the end of the day with our to-do list mostly undone, exclaiming that the days just aren't long enough to accomplish all that we set out to do? Why does it seem like there's not enough of us to go around?

The Hectic Pace of Life

Anxiety has become a common experience as we rush to catch up and feel depressed because we never do. Serenity is that elusive quality that would imply living at less than breakneck speed with occasional opportunities to stop and smell the roses, read a good book or marvel at a glorious sunset. But rarely do we find moments to reflect and catch our breath.

How did we ever get into such a hurry? We've learned to talk fast, eat fast and maybe even sleep in a hurry. Some things in life, however, suffer if we attempt them at top speed: family, conversation, worship, meals, friendships. If we rush through them, we risk alienating ourselves from God and from those around us. As I (Ellen) look back on the years when my children were in grade school, there are two words that I regret having spoken often: *Hurry up!* It's ironic that I used them to prod my children, given that I'm not always on time myself. In retrospect, the unhurried times I spent with my children were always the best.

Although it may not be the case for you, we've noticed that feeling stressed—and complaining about it—has become almost fashionable. The feeling that "my life's out of control" can be highly contagious. Stress can become a monster that we've helped to create, trying to convince ourselves that we really are busy, working hard and pulling our weight. It may be what has been described as the "hurry sickness," affecting our health, emotions and relationships. We may even forget why we are in such a rush or what we are hoping to accomplish. Some women seem to fear a sense of restlessness if they were ever to get caught up enough to have a few moments of quiet reflection.

Expectations of Perfection

Norm Wright cautions us that "perfectionism is a thief. It promises rewards but steals joy and satisfaction." We agree, but it's a struggle not to get caught up in society's low tolerance of imperfection. Some of the stresses we feel result from striving for unrealistic perfection, and this sets us up for even more dissatisfaction. Many of us have sought affirmation and appreciation from people around us, only to find that we end up disappointed. God never intended for us to be driven by the expectations of others, although that's the way many of us live.

Perhaps we sometimes place stringent expectations on ourselves. If we're married, we may feel we must be the perfect wife—attractive, loving and efficient—as we seek to meet our husband's physical and emotional needs, decorate our homes à la Martha Stewart, cook like a gourmet chef and entertain with ease and flair. We pay the bills, balance the budget and run endless errands. Some of us plan the family vacations and take tennis lessons. Grandma didn't have to worry about many of these responsibilities.

Unrealistic expectations affect our parenting as well. If our child is struggling in any area, we fear that we aren't doing our job adequately. We read books, get confused by all the conflicting theories and messages, and wonder why it isn't enough to affirm children when they're good and discipline them when they misbehave. We may think we have to produce the brightest and best children who are happy and well-adjusted and excel in every available opportunity. Consequently we arrange activities, lessons and experiences—and then spend so much time in the car that we come to think we could replace our home with a parking lot.

After years of hauling around children, pets and groceries, Darlene's van sputtered to a stop. She told her husband that she was ready for new wheels, but he didn't realize how big a change she wanted until they got to the car dealer and she fell in love with a foreign sports car. Darlene's husband pointed out, "Honey, this seven-passenger van over here has a luggage rack and captain chairs, all for the same price as the sports car."

She glared at him and snapped, "I don't like it."

"But why not?" her husband inquired.

Darlene replied, "It has 'Mother' written all over it!"

As much as we hate to admit it, when we hastily agree to any and all of our children's activity requests, we will likely put high mileage on ourselves as well as our cars.

Misleading Messages

Today women are often encouraged to believe that they can have good marriages, raise delightful children and complete graduate degrees, all before they reach thirty. We need to hear that life is usually long enough to accomplish several dreams, *but not all at once.* If a graduate degree is desired immediately, children may be postponed a few years; if starting a family first is the decision, further schooling may be postponed until the children are of school age. Women who try to have it both ways often feel frustrated and disappointed.

While growing up in China, I (Joan) dreamed of four careers! The "probable" ones involved nursing and psychology; loftier goals included a career in the diplomatic corps and being a foreign correspondent. As it turned out, I completed my nursing education in time to work in that field while my husband, Jim, completed medical school and OB-GYN residency training. When our children came along, I was thankful to be able to work only minimally outside the home until our youngest child, Jill, was in school full days. Then I pursued graduate work in psychology. This ultimately led to a counseling practice as well as teaching developmental psychology and family studies at a Christian college. I feel fulfilled in both sequences of my professional life, and I accept the fact that four careers in one lifetime just wasn't realistic! Writing a book wasn't even on my list until I met Ellen. Each phase of life brings surprises, challenges and choices, but there's not enough of us to attempt to do it all.

The Time and Energy Crunch

As we wrote this book, we dealt with pressures of time management ourselves. After working on it for two years, we felt relieved to deliver the manuscript to our publisher—on time! We expected that some changes would be necessary, but we didn't know how substantial they needed to be until we received our editors' comments. As we read through their observations, we began to see that our first draft had taken off a bit like a runaway train.

Though we felt overwhelmed, we realized that the editors' comments were a valuable gift, and that revising the manuscript would provide you with a much better book. "Rewriting," according to William Zinsser, instructor of writing at Yale, "is the essence of writing; it's where the game is won or lost."[1]

We had been looking forward to a summer free of writing deadlines; now we were faced with exactly the opposite. Over the summer we not only rewrote the book but also encountered other unforeseen events. Joan's father died in June, and her family also welcomed a new grandchild. Ellen's husband suffered a serious bicycle accident that put him in the hospital with a broken jaw and a broken wrist. For several weeks she didn't even think about this book while she cared for her husband's needs. These unexpected events presented us with further chances to practice what we preach. Thanks to God's help and the prayers of our families and friends, we reached our goal.

Boundary Confusion

Boundaries—or more likely a lack of them—are a huge source of frustration in many women's lives. If you find it difficult to say no or to state what you honestly think or feel about something, chances are that boundaries are a challenge for you.

One young college student who stayed with us (Joan and Jim) for a short time seemed oblivious to appropriate boundaries. She freely wandered in and out of our bedroom as if she were still living in a college dorm. She reminded me of a college roommate who borrowed clothing, shoes, books and records without ever inquiring whether I might have had plans for those items. She must have assumed that forgiveness is easier to get than permission. How do we deal with neighbors, friends and family who appear to have little regard for our space, time and belongings? Unresolved boundary issues leave us feeling frustrated and depleted.

Disappointment and Loss

Losses come in all shapes and sizes. Some are sudden, some are gradual. Some involve our family, some involve our health. Most of us don't have to live very long, though, before we experience a significant disappointment or loss of some kind. My (Ellen's) husband faced one such loss. When Jim was twenty-eight he was diagnosed with diabetes, and he has been insulin-dependent ever since. The months leading up to the diagnosis were stressful because he was tired and didn't feel himself, but neither one of us understood why. The diagnosis itself was stressful because it left us both in a mild state of shock. The months immediately following the diagnosis were stressful because Jim was learning how to manage his condition, while I was busy preparing foods that would help him keep his body chemistry controlled.

Sometimes we forget how wonderfully God has made our bodies until we develop a problem such as diabetes. Jim and I never gave much thought to how the pancreas works until Jim's pancreas stopped producing insulin. When it did, Jim learned how to manage the tasks that his pancreas originally managed by testing his blood sugar several times a day, controlling diet and exercise, and taking regular injections of insulin.

Diabetes has dictated certain circumstances in Jim's life that he never would have chosen, and it took a while for both of us to come to terms with his loss of freedom in certain areas. For example, whenever we go out to eat, he needs to excuse himself after he orders so that he can test his blood and take the appropriate amount of insulin. Or if he decides to go biking—his favorite exercise—he first needs to take into account where his blood sugar level is at that particular time. He also carries

Life Savers with him wherever he goes, just in case his blood sugar level goes too low.

Throughout those challenging months we were thankful for the help and encouragement of family and friends while we settled into new ways of doing things. Jim's diagnosis, now over twenty years ago, required him to develop a few extra routines, but thanks to his self-discipline, God's help and good medical technology, he's presently fit and healthy.

Some women experience loss when they or their husband unexpectedly lose a job. When Sally inherited the care of her mother who has Alzheimer's, the plans she had made for her empty nest years were suddenly put on hold. Instead of being free to travel and pursue a second career, Sally felt confined because she couldn't let her mother out of her sight. When disappointment and loss of any kind come our way, we find ourselves face to face with the reality that there just isn't enough to go around. How do we find the courage, strength and hope to keep going?

Family Challenges

Family challenges are great consumers of time and energy, at any stage of life. Early concerns might surface as leftover issues from our families of origin. This could include a woman's difficulty trusting her husband because of a parent's infidelity or a husband's resistance to sharing decision-making responsibility because of an overly controlling mother. We may also struggle with balancing all the relationships within our extended families. Finding enough time and energy to go around is difficult when both sets of parents want the newlyweds to spend Christmas with them. Later concerns commonly include a struggling marriage or a rebellious adolescent. Although our families bring us lots of joy, at times they stretch us to our limits.

When my (Joan's) children were school age, Jim was often away from home about a hundred hours a week, delivering babies literally night and day. Though I tried to make the most of the time we did have together as a family, it was difficult to be the "resident parent" stuck with all the tough stuff like discipline, enforcing rules, supervising chores, motivating homework and music practice, promoting character development, taking advantage of teachable moments, and on and on. It was easy to be resentful when Dad came home just in time to hop into the station wagon as we took off on vacation, or when he arrived on the scene just in time to enjoy guests after the house and yard were ready, food prepared and kids cleaned and polished. It was never my goal to become a "superwoman," but at times that was my necessary survival mode. I was fully aware of my mounting resentment and sometimes expressed it.

I just hoped that when the kids grew up they wouldn't remember me as the ogre I sometimes felt I was becoming. I would rather have had more time to enjoy them. I hoped Jan and Winsor would remember all the times I put on my ice skates to skate with them on the frozen swamp in the backyard, or the times I played tennis with them. I hoped they'd remember the countless soccer and basketball games, track meets and tennis matches that I attended, even after our "dessert" child, Jill, arrived; she was often there with me, bundled up in a stroller. Thankfully, I believe they have. I also have a deep appreciation for single moms—because I often felt like one.

Trying to Go It Alone

Dependency is not a popular word or concept in our culture; it flies in the face of ideas we are encouraged to believe and accept as desirable. Not only are we subjected to a great variety of external and internal expectations, but we sometimes expect ourselves to meet them *on our own*. Have skill and performance eclipsed our connections with each other?

Some of our unhealthy stress results from society's emphasis on self-sufficiency and individualism. Under such pressure we may be driven either to a state of neediness that leads to despair *or* to a state of neediness that helps us experience grace through relationships with God and others.

I (Ellen) recall a Sunday afternoon when Chad and Nate were six and four. As we chauffeured my husband to the airport for a business trip, Chad spoke those five words that no mother wants to hear: "Mommy, my tummy feels funny." Of course! Moms with husbands who travel know that it's not unusual for kids to get sick when Dad's gone. Throughout that day, Chad's funny feeling developed into genuine illness, and in the middle of the night I was still up taking care of him.

> *The ultimate step in the process of stress prevention is changing the way we view ourselves and our place in the world. If I can make these changes, I can be freed from my captivity to unwanted stress.*
>
> RICHARD E. ECKER

Feeling lonely and stressed at 2:00 a.m., I called my sister, Gail, who lived next door. After explaining my situation through tears, I said, "Would you please come over? I'm really struggling!"

Gail showed up at my back door five minutes later and simply asked, "What can I do?"

I replied, "If you'll just sleep here for the rest of the night, I'll feel better knowing that someone's with me." Her presence meant a great deal to me that night, even though she was asleep. Just knowing that she was in my house helped me to feel more secure. It's difficult to face pressure when we feel like we're alone.

Changing Seasons of Life

Have you already identified with some of the challenges we've mentioned? Perhaps the following scenarios from life's seasons encapsulate why there's not enough of you to go around at certain times.

☐ You're a new wife who is attempting to balance time and energy among your husband, parents and in-laws, friends and a job. There's so much to learn all at once and you never served an apprenticeship. Because of our highly mobile society, you may also have moved far away from a supportive system of family, friends and familiarity. Some days are better than others!

☐ You're single, and it seems as if everyone else is getting married. A short while ago you were a college student, but graduation suddenly transformed you into a "single." At your workplace you are sometimes expected to carry more of the load than women with children because fellow workers reason that you don't have to rush home to a family. At the same time, you sense that your community and church have much more to offer families than they have to offer singles.

☐ You're a new mom, and your roles are multiplying. You're a wife, mother, daughter, friend, neighbor and church member. Finding balance in your life is becoming more complicated. You realize that much of parenting is learned by experience, but we all have to begin with a first child. As Alvin Toffler notes, "Parenthood remains the single greatest preserve of the amateur."

☐ Your children attend three different schools—one's in high school, one's in junior high, one's in grade school. You're receiving phone calls begging you to be involved in PTA, your child's classroom, Sunday school, soccer tournaments and fundraisers. You and your husband are like two ships passing in the night. Some days it seems as though you're on a merry-go-round that won't quit, and you'd like to call out, "Stop! I want to get off!"

☐ Your children are going off to college. Since expenses are higher than ever, you're working more hours than you'd like. You wish you could spend more time with friends—you long for a breakfast or lunch out so that you could really *connect* with another woman. You've scarcely had a chance to evaluate how all of the changes are affecting you personally.

☐ You're helping your daughter, a recent college graduate, hunt for an apartment while you're also calling every retirement center within a ten-mile radius. Your parents need to move out of their house because they're having difficulty with routine tasks like cooking and cleaning. You hadn't realized that their needs would coincide with your children's needs.

If we've never taken a look at how each of these seasons of our lives affects the big picture, we may have difficulty making sense of things along the way.

Why Do We Want More to Go Around?

We want peace of heart. We want more time to do the things that are important. We want to grow in confidence so that we can live beyond ourselves, reaching out to a hurting world. We want to learn how to say no and how to set boundaries. We want to find hope for the times when there just isn't enough to go around. We want more—and better—time for our families and friends. And we want to understand how all these things fit into a purposeful life.

These are all admirable things to seek after, and they can be found. We believe that if after reading a book we come away with two or three helpful thoughts or ideas, the book was worth our time and money. We're hoping that you'll find a lot more than two or three in this book. Although the people who appear throughout the pages of this book represent a variety of families, stages and backgrounds, one thing that they have in common is that they found more to go around. You can too.

Reflection Questions

1. What is one pressure or frustration that prompts you to say, "There isn't enough of me to go around"?

2. How have you dealt with these kinds of frustrations in the past? What helped? What didn't?

3. Do you identify with any of the scenarios in this chapter? Explain.

4. Look at one Bible character who felt like there wasn't enough of her to go around: Mary (Luke 1:26-56). How did she deal with her confusion and questions, and how were her needs met?

5. Read and reflect on John 6:1-35. In what ways did the characters in these verses move from "not enough" to "enough"?

6. What is one expectation—of yourself, of others, of God—that you may need to evaluate more intentionally?

7. What is one boundary issue that presents a challenge for you?

2

I Can't Do It All, and I Can't Do Life Alone

Some who attempted to do it all
were overwhelmed by their tasks and found
they could complete none of them.
They sought refuge by subtracting their sanity.

GAIL SHEEHY

*I*t was a chilly November morning, and I (Ellen) was out for my daily walk—one of my favorite times to think. Swirling around in my brain were the many—too many—roles I was trying to juggle: wife, mother of three sons, daughter, sister, friend, piano teacher of twenty-eight students, Bible study leader, writer, officer in a state music organization, accompanist, string ensemble member at church. I'd felt overwhelmed before, but this time it was different. I was beginning to feel trapped—as if there were no way out. I knew that I could cut down on some of my activities, but with the expense of two kids in college, I couldn't imagine being able to decrease my teaching load. I'd probably need to teach *more*, not less, I thought.

I wanted to invest more time in God's Word and people's lives; these were becoming increasingly important to me. But the idea of massively restructuring my life left me feeling overwhelmed. Even if I could trim back on teaching, the thought of explaining it all to my piano students and their families made me shiver. I felt so overwhelmed as I walked south on Driving Park Road that I pleaded, out loud, "God, I just can't do all this anymore. It's too much. Please help me!"

In December of that year, yet another challenge surfaced. One night after dinner my husband, Jim, explained that he and his business partner had concluded that their business could no longer support them both. They agreed that something had to change.

I sat stunned, thinking, *I was praying for a lighter work schedule, not a heavier one.* Not knowing exactly *what* the restructuring of their business would mean, I braced myself for the worst.

Overwhelmed? You're Not Alone

You wouldn't be reading this book if you had never had the feeling that there wasn't enough of you to go around. We've all felt that way. But feeling it and dealing with it are two different things. Many of us feel overwhelmed, but not all of us have *accepted* the fact that we can't be or do it all.

Sometimes when we encounter difficult situations, we try to handle things ourselves. We're a little like the two-year-old who, determined to dress himself, exclaims, "Me do it myself!" After several frustrating, time-consuming efforts, he gives up in a fit of rage (the infamous two-year-old temper tantrum) when he finally realizes that his awkwardly buttoned coat has become a straitjacket and he can't get anywhere with boots on the wrong feet. Only then is he willing to accept any assistance. Sometimes as adults we discover that we're acting the same way. We're trying—very hard—to do things ourselves, but there's just not enough to go around.

There are various ways we attempt to deal with feelings of being overwhelmed. We may live by the faulty assumption that we really have to do it all, so we continue to try harder and harder, run faster and faster. This leaves us feeling enslaved to the expectations and demands of others. Underneath we lack confidence to thoughtfully evaluate our lives and make intentional choices about the best use of our time and gifts. We end up feeling frustrated, exhausted and burned out.

Relying on God has to begin all over again every day as if nothing had yet been done.

C. S. LEWIS

Another response to feeling over-whelmed by the pressures and demands of life is to give up too soon, believing that if we can't do it all there's no use try-ing. We may be tempted to check out. And then we fall into a variety of unhealthy habits to compound our sense of defeat in a downward spiral.

A life-giving alternative is to acknowledge the responsibili-ties and challenges of life and accept the fact that we can't do it all on our own. That's the first step in turning our hearts toward God, seeking his presence and relying on him moment by moment.

Experiencing God's Presence and Help

Finding enough to go around is not solely a matter of time management. It has much more to do with understanding the meaning of our life, discovered through a relationship with

God. Made in his image (Genesis 1:27), we were created with the capacity to know him and communicate with him.

God also gave us the freedom to choose our direction in life, which determines whether we live in purposeful pursuit of God or intentional avoidance of his loving pursuit of us. We can come to him and experience abundant life (John 10:10), or we can run away, as Francis Thompson eloquently describes:

> I fled Him, down the nights and down the days;
> I fled Him, down the arches of the years.
> I fled Him down the labyrinthine ways
> of my own mind; and in the midst of tears,
> I hid from Him.[1]

It's often our insecurities and fears, our difficult marriage, our failures, our challenging children that initially bring us running into God's arms. We know that we need him. What we discover is that he provides not only help for these immediate needs but also a life-giving relationship when we are reconciled to God through Christ.

Come near to God and he will come near to you. JAMES 4:8   Two biblical women whose lives were changed through their relationship with Christ are examples for us all. Both women had incredible needs—the first through no choice of her own, the second through some poor choices.

Mark 5:24-34 recounts that Jesus was on his way to Jairus's house when a woman approached him from behind and touched him. This was not just any touch from any woman in the crowd—it was a touch of faith from a needy woman. The woman had bled for twelve years, suffered greatly and spent all she had on medical help. She had a period that just wouldn't quit, and she had exhausted all her resources. The woman's posture with Jesus was distinctly unassuming; in fact, today's culture might have suggested that she pursue assertiveness training. The ostracized woman didn't come before Jesus and request an audience; she came up behind him and reached out to touch his clothes, believing that a touch of his clothing would be enough to heal her.

The instant she touched Jesus' garment, two things happened: her bleeding stopped, and Jesus knew that "power had gone out from him." Jesus turned around. He knew exactly where this woman was, just as he always knows exactly where *we* are. He asked, "Who touched my clothes?" Jesus waited until the woman fell at his feet—the place we all go when we see him for who he is and realize how much we need him—and timidly told the truth about herself.

Once the woman knelt at Jesus' feet, notice how Jesus elevated her as a person.

> He wanted to be to her something more than a healer: He wanted to be her Savior and Friend as well. He wanted her to look into His face, feel His tenderness, and hear His loving words of assurance. By the time He finished speaking to her, she experienced something more than physical healing. He called her "daughter" and sent her on her way with a benediction of peace (Mark 5:34). To "be made whole" meant much more than receiving mere physical healing. Jesus had given her spiritual healing as well![2]

Jesus wasn't interested only in getting this woman out of a jam. He was interested in having a personal relationship with her, as he is with each of us.

A second woman who discovered that Jesus desired a life-giving relationship with her met him at the well of Sychar. If you've ever feared that choices you made in the past exclude you from having a relationship with God in the present, this story is for you. When Jesus initiated a conversation with the woman at the well (John 4:1-26), he knew that she was a Samaritan—an ethnic group despised by Jewish people—and a morally loose woman at that.

As Jesus approached the woman, asking for a drink of water, the woman's expectation may have been more sexual than spiritual, since, as we learn later, she had been divorced five times and was presently living with a sixth man. Even though Jesus began telling her who he was and that he could give her living water (the reason he pursues us all), she was initially unable to see beyond the material nature of water and water jars to the spiritual issues of her heart.

But Jesus went straight to the reality of her life when he asked her to go get her husband. When the woman attempted to deceive him by saying that she had no husband, Jesus knew the whole truth of her sexual history and spoke it to her directly. The woman quickly saw Jesus' prophetic abilities and abruptly directed the conversation toward general spirituality and religious disputes. After she presented her strong opinions on what she thought was the proper place to worship, Jesus stressed the importance of *how* we worship—in spirit and in truth.

Concluding their conversation, Jesus identified himself to the woman as the Christ. All of a sudden she realized that although Jesus had asked her for a drink of water, he himself was the Fountain of Life! In her excitement, she left her water pot and ran back to her town.

This woman, who had just been lovingly confronted with the sin in her life, had every reason to run away in shame, and yet she returned to Jesus, bringing other people with her. She knew that Jesus has something to offer her—something that was beyond the scope of her resources. What a beautiful picture of how God's grace reaches out to each of us. Even though we all have sinned and fallen short of God's glory (Romans 3:23), God showed his great love by sending Christ to die for us while we were still sinners (Romans 5:8).

Left to our own resources we can never muster enough righteousness to go around. But through faith in Jesus' death and resurrection, God clothes us with *his* righteousness. He has done for us what we cannot do for ourselves.

Jesus' pursuit of the woman's soul is encouraging to us all. He cut across barriers of gender, race and morals to communicate to the Samaritan woman who he was (God), what he had to offer (eternal life) and how she could receive it (faith). He is not discriminating or prejudiced; he is a God who pursues a relationship with each one of us, even though we all present our own obstacles.

It's comforting to know that the God who made us and knows everything about us is someone we can know as our Father. Once we realize that God has been seeking us and we respond to him in faith, we'll find ourselves desiring to spend time with him just as we would want to develop any meaningful relationship. Two of the ways we can do that are reading the Bible and praying.

The Bible — God's Communication to Us

At this point you may be thinking, *I'm not sure you understand. I'm a busy woman. Where would I ever find time to read the Bible?* Well, finding time to read the Bible is not unlike finding time to eat. Even in the midst of a particularly busy week, it's not likely that we would say, "I think I'll eat only once this week—I'm just too busy." We eat every day—usually several times—to nourish our body. If we didn't, we'd run out of energy and

strength. Just as we eat food because we need physical sustenance, we read the Bible because we need spiritual sustenance.
Once we discover that God's Word is a feast for our soul, we
begin asking ourselves, *Why would I ever want to go without it?*

We can experience God's Word in many forms, but usually
we need to start with personal reading of the Bible. I (Ellen)
enjoy using the *Two-Year Daily Reading and Prayer Bible*
(Zondervan). If you're a novice (don't think you're the only
one—there are many people who have never read through the
Bible), reading the whole Bible straight through may seem very
daunting, so you may want to start with an individual book of
the Bible. If you're feeling discouraged, you may want to begin
in the Psalms, where you will identify with writers who express
their deepest pain but usually conclude on a note of triumph
and praise. "In whatever strange or common situation, I have
never failed to find a psalm that met me there."[3]

There are many creative ways to fit God's Word into everyday life. You may want to keep a small Bible in your car to read
during little "adjoinings of time"—while you wait for your
child at soccer practice or your husband at the train station.
Posting encouraging verses inside cabinet doors or on mirrors
will brighten your day. Isaiah 26:3 or 2 Timothy 1:6 may
become a favorite. Even though we're busy women, we can find
approaches that fit our lifestyle.

When my (Ellen) first two sons were young toddlers, I
wanted to read through the whole Bible but couldn't imagine
how I'd find the time. One day I prayed, "God, if you'll arrange
for both Chad and Nate to nap after lunch *at the same time,* I'll
try to read through the Bible in a year." God graciously
answered my prayer. It didn't work *every* day, but it worked
most days. As I read through the Bible that year, my soul felt
rich, and I was strengthened for the demands of each day.

Prayer — Our Lifeline to God

If there were ever a person in the history of the world who felt as though everyone wanted a piece of him, it must have been Jesus. Everywhere he went, people wanted to talk to him, follow him, eat with him or be healed by him. One man even came to see him in the middle of the night. People wanted him to speak at their synagogues and come to their banquets.

How did Jesus keep his sense of balance? You might respond, "Well, Jesus was God." Yes, but he was also a man who got hungry, thirsty and tired as we do. It was time spent with his Father that kept Jesus going, and those times were his priority. "But Jesus often withdrew to lonely places and prayed" (Luke 5:16). Prayer is also our lifeline to God.

> *Prayer is much more than giving God our list of needs. . . . It is not a magical way of getting what we want. Prayer is to get us into the position of willingness to receive what God wants.*
> LLOYD JOHN OGILVIE

"Prayer is more than just sitting in a quiet place and mumbling some prayers. It is fellowship with God and that means dwelling in His presence."[4] Robert C. Roberts, a Christian writer concerned with spiritual formation, suggests trying to find a comfortable position but not one that is sleep-inducing, in a place that is relatively free from distractions. He also suggests deciding on a set time and duration for prayer, focusing on Scripture and allowing it to be a dialogue with God.

In addition to times of structured prayer, we can keep a running conversation with God throughout the day. Pray when you're breastfeeding your baby, while you're ironing or when you're driving (if you're alone—it's not nearly as dangerous or distracting as talking on a cell phone!).

My (Joan's) three-mile walking route becomes a prayer list,

as I pray for the same people at approximately the same place every day. Mailboxes, trees and houses serve as reminders of my family and friends. For other prayer times, writing out a list of requests and answers in a prayer journal helps me to concentrate. Keeping a record of answers to prayer reminds me of God's faithfulness when life gets discouraging. We all know that it does. It also helps me to cultivate a grateful heart.

Brother Lawrence, a seventeenth-century monk, found God's presence to be real even as he scrubbed pots and pans in a monastery kitchen. He took an everyday chore and turned it into time spent with God—something we can all do. One woman tells us that every time she goes to the water cooler at her office, she's learned to be reminded of her need for the "living water." Following Christ means allowing the truth of God's Word to be worked out in my life, affecting everything I think, say and do. Developing an intentional "God-consciousness" heightens our awareness of God's presence in the everyday details of our life. We begin to experience God sightings that encourage and energize us amidst the mundane routines of our days.

> *As much as God wants me to find the time to come away to pray for more than a few moments, he knows that may not happen every day, at least while my children are still preschoolers. So in the meantime, I think, he'd like to do life with me, to be next to me as I drive the carpool, meet with a client or wash the dishes.*
>
> KERI WYATT KENT

We can spend moments with God anytime, anywhere. My (Joan's) favorite times are by a rushing mountain stream near Buena Vista, Colorado, where time alone with God renews my perspective on life. I (Ellen) never was a morning person while growing up (getting to school on time was always a challenge), but now I savor the early morning hours. I agree with Benjamin Franklin, who said, "The morning hour has gold in its hand." The time I spend reading the Bible and praying, while the house is still quiet and I enjoy a hot cup of coffee with vanilla creamer, is a gift that keeps on giving throughout the day.

Caring for Our Soul

Many of us identify with this awareness: "We have a calendar that is full but a heart that is withering, shrinking, unable to care deeply or experience pleasure feelings."[5] If we neglect the care of our soul and fail to nurture the spiritual dimension of our life, we become prey to the maladies of our time—stress, anxiety, burnout and depression. Experiencing what is described in Deuteronomy 28:65, "an anxious mind, eyes weary with longing, and a despairing heart," we long for a sense of serenity to withstand life's inevitable storms.

> *Take time and trouble to keep yourself spiritually fit. Bodily fitness has certain value but spiritual fitness is essential both for this present life and for the life to come.*
> 1 TIMOTHY 4:8 (PHILLIPS)

Perhaps we've wistfully observed this quality in others but haven't experienced it ourselves.

We are not suggesting that women who spend time with God regularly will never be depressed, anxious or stressed, for we all experience those feelings from time to time in varying degrees. It has a lot to do with our circumstances and our temperament. Rather, we acknowledge that since the storms of life are inevitable, it's tremendously comforting to know that when we seek God we will find him. And when we find him, we're pleased to discover that along with his presence comes his peace.

If we depend only on *our* resources, we'll never have enough to go around. We must accept that we can't be or do it all and that we need to seek God's presence. As we spend time with him, we begin to understand who he is, what he did, why he came, how we should live and what he can do for us. As the disciples learned when Jesus fed the five thousand, we learn that not only does he provide enough bread to go around, but he is the Bread of Life.

> The self can never cope with the ultimate issues of life because it was never designed to "go it alone."
>
> DR. ARCHIBALD D. HART

Back to Ellen's outcry to God during her morning walk: Although I had no less responsibility after I cried out to God than before, something changed. I knew that he had heard me. I had cried out to God other times when circumstances seemed impossible, and he had heard me and helped me. I had experienced the truth of Psalm 34:4-5: "I sought the LORD, and he answered me; he delivered me from all my fears. Those who look to him are radiant; their faces are never covered with shame." I had lived long enough to know that overwhelming situations rarely have instant solutions, but I also knew that coming to God was the place to start. I needed to accept that I couldn't handle all the demands myself (although I'd tried); I needed to ask for God's help. The cry for help that I prayed to God that November morning proved to be the beginning of an interesting year.

Jim told me of his business struggles in December. The next five months of waiting were difficult. Amidst my fears, tears and prayers, however, God surprised me. My husband and his business partner ended up selling their business, and God provided a new job for Jim. Both of these provisions enabled me to reduce my teaching schedule significantly. Notifying my piano students and their families *was* difficult—more like gut-wrenching, actually—but I was thankful to be freed up to pursue things that were growing more important to me.

And then I became overwhelmed in a different way. I was overwhelmed with joy because of a reversal that had nothing to do with me and everything to do with God.

Reflection Questions

1. Describe one time in your life when you felt your need for God especially keenly.

2. What time of day works best for you to spend quiet moments alone with God? What's a good location?

3. What is one way God has helped you in a life challenge?

4. Read John 4:4-29 and Luke 8:40-48. Put yourself in the place of the woman at the well and the woman who touched Jesus. If you were standing face to face with Jesus, what question would you like to ask him? What would you ask him for?

5. Read Hebrews 4:12, Colossians 3:16, Romans 10:17 and Psalm 119:11, 37, 130. How does the Bible make a difference in our lives?

6. Tell of an answer to prayer in the past that continues to encourage you even now.

7. What is one way that you might become more aware of God's presence in the daily routine of your life?

3

Confident Women Have More to Go Around

God does not love me because I have worth
but I have worth because God loves me
MARTIN LUTHER

As a student nurse, I (Joan) often felt overwhelmed by the responsibilities thrust on me at the age of seventeen. I was faced with life-and-death crises daily. After one year of nurse's training, I was given "charge duty" of an entire floor of the hospital on the night shift. I'll never forget that summer night. One of my patients was a critically ill asthmatic college girl needing respiratory treatments. While I struggled with the complicated equipment to which she was hooked up, I listened for the man across the hall. He had been brought to the hospital intoxicated, and my worst fear was that he would awake from his stupor and fly into a rage. At the same time, a terminally ill cancer patient was close to death, and her family needed a chaplain. Moments like that were frightening, and I longed to feel more confident.

Why Do We Need Confidence?

Confidence helps us decide what we must do, what we might do and what we won't be able to do—at least not today. We all need confidence to make the nitty-gritty decisions about what's most important in our daily life, and we also want confidence to make the big decisions regarding career, marriage and children. In order to help us preserve energy and sanity, we also need confidence to establish appropriate boundaries in our relationships. Otherwise we may feel that our lives are out of control or that they're being run by others.

When we lack confidence, a pervasive sense of inadequacy cripples every aspect of our life. We feel that we don't have enough to go around.

Confidence Begins with a Relationship

We're surrounded by women who say that they need confidence but don't have it. Our need becomes a sales hook: commercials tell us we can find confidence in hair color or self-help books or a new exercise program. It's easy to get caught up in these ideas even though all through the Bible people are described as confident when they trust the Lord, cling to him and follow him.

When someone wants to become a pilot, in addition to gaining knowledge and skill through lessons, he or she must log in flying time. In much the same way, we grow in confidence by logging experiences of believing and following Christ and experiencing his faithfulness.

As a college freshman in 1970, I (Ellen) wanted to attend the Urbana Missions Convention. Because my parents were paying for my college education (as well as paying Dr. Hanson to put braces on my younger siblings' teeth), I hesitated to ask them for yet more money. I decided to ask God to provide money for me to attend the missions conference.

Several weeks later my mom called me at college to say that the company I had worked for during the summer had just inquired about my last paycheck. According to their records I had never cashed it. By mistake I had left the uncashed check at home, sitting on a

> A confident woman does not run around looking for herself, because she has learned to accept who she is physically, emotionally, and mentally.
> INGRID TROBISCH

stack of paycheck stubs. When my mom told me the amount of the check, I realized that not only was it enough money for me to attend the conference, but it included enough for round-trip transportation.

My confidence grew when I experienced firsthand that God cares for me enough to hear me and provide for me. That experience took place more than thirty years ago but was only one of many times I have found God's help amidst uncertainty. Sometimes I have looked to him, sometimes I have not. But each time I have turned to him, my confidence has grown.

In many areas of life it is difficult to figure out how to do something *right* without first understanding how it might go *wrong*. Growing in confidence is like this. So it's helpful for us to understand some of the obstacles to confidence: distorted beliefs, critical messages and misplaced confidence.

Distorted Beliefs

Although confidence includes self-acceptance, we run into trouble if we think that the world revolves around us. Psalm 36 explains that if we do not look past ourselves, we become self-absorbed and increasingly insecure. This can happen to women who are obsessed with having a perfect body. Going far beyond healthy habits of exercise and good eating, we make the health club our second home, to the detriment of marriage, family and even character. It is possible for women to become so intent on having a beautiful body that it becomes a form of idolatry.

Making confidence our main goal in life can actually make us more insecure. We become so preoccupied, self-consumed and self-conscious that we don't think of much beyond ourselves. If we focus our eyes first on God, though, we can walk confidently down the path that leads to a full life.

Remember playing hide-and-seek as a child? We waited until Mom's car was out of the driveway and down the street, then we begged Dad to let us turn off all the lights in the house. (Mothers don't like this game because they think it's not safe. *They're right.*) After we talked Dad into it, he gave us the usual warnings—go slowly, don't run, watch out for the younger siblings. We never knew who was going to come creeping around the next corner and scare us half out of our minds. Whenever it was our turn to hide, we got so excited that we almost forgot to breathe when we heard footsteps coming near our hiding place. Although we always had great fun, the game often ended abruptly with someone crying because in the dark they had bumped into a wall, a post or a sibling.

We loved playing hide-and-seek, but it really was hard to move confidently in the dark. Our movements were awkward and uncertain because we couldn't see where we were going. Focusing only on ourselves is a lot like turning off the lights. We tend to stumble around, and eventually someone gets hurt. When we choose to focus on God, though, we discover that we can move freely and confidently in his light.

Another distortion is *not realizing how much God loves us.* We all feel occasional embarrassment or regret over something we've done or something we've said—that's healthy—but some of us live with continual shame and regret over who we *are.*

Eliza struggled with much more than a sense of inadequacy. She thought she was downright worthless, and she wasn't sure that she wanted to live. Although Eliza's feelings had a lot to do with loneliness and isolation, she thought she felt that way because she had no value. Whenever she felt terrible, she'd attempt to drown her sorrows in alcohol, which left her feeling even worse.

When family members stopped making excuses for Eliza's drinking and destructive behavior, refusing to play supportive roles, Eliza began to experience the consequences. Her misery prompted her to seek help, and encouraging things began to happen. Through some of the people around her, Eliza realized she had worth in God's sight, and through the Bible she discovered she could have a new identity based on his righteousness

When we begin to see that God's love is the foundation of our worth, we will not think more lowly of ourselves than we ought. That's dignity. But we will also not think more highly of ourselves than we ought. That's humility. As we keep our eyes focused on God, our confidence grows both in dignity and humility.

> *Ironically, when we focus on ourselves we cannot see ourselves. We in this century devote an incredible amount of energy to peering inward, trying to find the truth about ourselves. We have lost the fear of God, which before our eyes acts as a true reflector through which we can rightly see ourselves. Focusing on God puts ourselves into focus.*
> KATHLEEN B. NIELSON

Critical Messages

The level of confidence we experience now is certainly related to our family experiences from childhood on. Some of the con-

> *The fact that the King of all creation found me so valuable that he paid for my membership into heaven by sacrificing the life of his Son should have a profound impact on my feeling of worth and self-esteem.*
> ROBERT G. BARNES JR.

fidence builders that healthy families promote are love, acceptance, traditions, personal responsibility and respect for individuals. "We use as our mirrors the significant people around us, an exclusive group of people that we look to for 'reflections.' The way they reflect back at us, or respond to us, gives us information as to how valuable we are and who we are."[1] It is not surprising, then, that women who grew up with critical parental messages don't seem to have enough confidence now. Growing in confidence means identifying any negative, distorted statements about ourselves that we have heard and internalized and replacing them with truth.

Cathy grew up believing that she'd never be good enough. As an adult she worked toward building confidence, but the fragile structure of her life came crashing down when her marriage ended abruptly. In her mid-forties and with two teenagers, she had financial concerns that compounded her sense of loss. Though she had maintained her teaching credentials, she hadn't taught for some years, and the thought of returning to the classroom filled her with panic. The excruciating rejection she felt from the divorce left her without the emotional energy to face the work of rebuilding her confidence. There didn't seem to be enough of anything to go around.

Five years after her divorce, however, Cathy was able to look back and see how much her confidence had grown. Although the agony of her marriage and divorce was something she never would have chosen, her dependence on God had given her more confidence, strength and hope than she ever could have imagined. She had been learning to identify the painful messages and hurts from her past and replace them with truth and hope from God's Word. With renewed confidence, she was able to pursue a fulfilling new career.

When we begin to believe the truth about who we are, God's grace liberates us from the critical messages or distorted beliefs by which we have been living.

Learning to identify and believe what is true, as opposed to what is false, and then choosing appropriate responses to that truth forms the core of our life restructuring process. And more truth-filled belief systems produce more stable lives.
SANDRA D. WILSON

Misplaced Confidence

We need to beware of putting our confidence in people, performance or possessions. As good as anything or anyone might be, the danger exists that we might depend too much on them for our sense of who we are or for our happiness. It can all be taken away very quickly and unexpectedly.

People. It's easy to become dependent on our life partner to give us much of our identity, especially if that person is a dynamic leader. When a woman loses her spouse she may find she has lost a huge piece of her identity, derived from her previous role as corporate wife or ministry partner. For her, getting on with life means discovering who she is and what God has for her to do in her own circle of influence.

A good marriage offers each individual a sense of constructive autonomy. The popular expression "your better half" betrays an unhelpful way of looking at a marriage relationship.

Another damaging view is the romantic notion movies promote: that love means not being able to define oneself apart from one's spouse—"not knowing where one began and the other left off." Instead our goal should be interdependence.

> *Don't put your confidence in powerful people; there is no help for you there. When their breathing stops, they return to the earth, and in a moment all their plans come to an end. But happy are those who have the God of Israel as their helper, whose hope is in the Lord their God.*
> PSALM 146:3-5 (NLT)

Living out our life through our children is another danger of misplaced confidence. Vicariously assuming their successes as our source of validation is unfair both to our children and to us. A mom who derives too much of her satisfaction from her child's performance actually sets herself up for greater loss during the empty-nest phase of her own life. If she is not comfortable with herself and where she is in life, she may attempt to live out her dreams and ambitions through her children. She may put pressure on them to hurry on to the next phase of their life, rushing into romance, marriage and parenting before they are ready.

We are reminded of Allison, who felt the expectations of her family to carry on the tradition of becoming a physician. Carried along by those expectations, she entered medical school. Allison's stress level mounted considerably, though, when she married and became pregnant during her residency. Since her husband had his own demanding career, consistent childcare became a challenge.

Three years after she joined a group practice, her second child arrived. She felt torn between career and family. Allison knew she'd feel guilty about wasting her education and expertise if she stayed home, but she was also feeling guilty about the amount of time she was spending away from her children. There wasn't enough of her to go around. Her dilemma was compounded by the discovery that her career did not seem to be as fulfilling as she had hoped.

It's unfortunate when a degree, a career or a performance becomes the foundation of our worth or identity. None of these pursuits are wrong in themselves, but they are never enough to validate our existence.

Performance. There is danger in narrowing our identity to the mere sense of what we do. An emphasis on doing rather than being may apply to our talents, abilities or vocation. Perhaps athletic or musical talent or ability has become our distinguishing feature. In some cases it is also our vocation—and then the potential for real loss is even greater.

Possessions. Another type of misplaced confidence is reliance on things—material possessions—to impart a sense of worth. Whether it's clothes, house or furnishings, this deceit has the potential of becoming a tyranny that grips like a vise and pulls us into vicious cycles of competition, jealousy and perpetual discontent. "Tell those who are rich in this present world not to be contemptuous of others, and not to rest the weight of their confidence on the transitory power of wealth but on the living God, who generously gives us everything for our enjoyment" (1 Timothy 6:17 Phillips).

Consider a few comments from some of the wealthiest men in history.

JOHN D. ROCKEFELLER: *"I have made many millions, but they have brought me no happiness."*

W. H. VANDERBILT: *"The care of $200,000,000 is enough to kill anyone. There is no pleasure in it."*

JOHN JACOB ASTOR: *"I am the most miserable man on earth."*

HENRY FORD: *"I was happier when doing a mechanic's job."*

ANDREW CARNEGIE: *"Millionaires seldom smile."*

From RANDY ALCORN, Money, Possessions and Eternity (*Wheaton, Ill.:* Tyndale House, 1989), p. 69.

Confidence Includes Understanding Myself

Although focusing *only* on ourselves fosters greater insecurity, *some* reflection on our life is healthy and worthwhile. "The unexamined life," Plato said, "is not worth living." How we perceive ourselves greatly determines how we live our life, so before we begin deciding how to order our days, we need to have some sense of who we are and what we're all about.

> *A strong sense of identity is necessary for a woman to keep her balance in her calling and work . . . it's about integrity, about staying true to this authentic personhood in the variety of life situations. . . .*
> *Jesus himself was the epitome of a person with a strong sense of personhood.*
> MARY ELLEN
> ASHCROFT

When Moses had serious confidence problems and said to God, "What if the people won't listen to me?" God answered him by asking, "What is that in your hand?" Moses had a staff in his hand, and God used it as a sign of Moses' authority (Exodus 4:2). If we're willing to trust God, he often takes what we have in our hands and uses it.

When the widow in 2 Kings 4 heard creditors knocking at her door, she ran to Elisha for help. Elisha asked her, "How can I help you? Tell me, what do you have in your house?" There's the question again—what do we have to work with? The widow had just a little oil, and God—through Elisha—stretched it not only to pay her debts but also to provide enough for her and her children to live on.

We all have different energy levels, sleep requirements, and various other resources and aptitudes; accepting this is necessary if we are to function optimally. Are you an early bird or a night owl? Not every one of us is a Type A, highly driven personality—thank goodness. Each of us needs to be aware of what energizes or depletes us; it differs according to each individual's personality. As we learn how to evaluate these issues, we'll preserve and extend our resources over the long haul. It's a matter of being ecological in a personal sense—so we'll have more to go around.

Take a few minutes to do a personal inventory. Putting our thoughts into words starts to bring clarity and perspective to our life, and when reviewed, what we've written can provide us with a measurement of our personal growth. Your answers to these questions will give you a better idea of what you have to work with.

SOCIAL: How do friends and family view or describe you? Ask for constructive feedback. Are you an introvert or an extrovert? Are you a leader or a follower? What is your customary role in relationships?

SPIRITUAL: Where are you in terms of your beliefs and faith development? How is your faith being integrated into your daily life? Is it a religion or a relationship with Jesus?

PSYCHOLOGICAL: How do you view yourself? What are you learning about yourself? Which of your personal traits do you want to continue to cultivate and which do you want to modify?

PHYSICAL: What are your physical characteristics? Are you making the most of the givens? Are there lifestyle changes you could make that would improve your overall health?

VOCATIONAL: How fulfilled are you in your current vocation, whether it's homemaking, a profession, a career or a combination? Is it a role you have chosen? Are your abilities being utilized? Are you thinking in terms of creative sequences and combinations of life callings?

Being aware of our abilities and limitations also helps free us from being driven by comparisons to others. "One of the greatest hindrances to becoming confident is to compare oneself with another person. If I am constantly looking sideways andcomparing myself with my friend, my sister, my neighbor, or even a woman of another country, chances are I will be miserable."[2] Life is not a competition, it's a journey. Although each of our journeys is unique, we can all find contentment as we focus on pleasing God, using wisely the gifts he has given us.

There are *some* givens that we have to accept (such as height and eye color), but in other areas we may become aware that we have more opportunities for personal growth than we ever realized. Throughout life we have the possibility of creatively discovering previously unused gifts and developing new skills if we're confident enough to do some experimentation and take a few risks.

Up until recent years, I (Ellen) had not done much public speaking, and when I did, I accepted speaking engagements with some trepidation. I had too many butterflies and not enough confidence. Several years ago I hired a coach to help me in this area, with encouraging results. My enjoyment in public speaking has increased, and although the butterflies have not flown away completely, they are now flying in formation.

Confidence Grows

Isn't it curious that some of the most confident women we know are women who have faced problems or experienced losses—some huge—and found that God is good and that he is enough? We all wish that such faith were a trait to be inherited or to be absorbed through osmosis, but it's not. Faith and confidence are qualities that are worked out in our relationship to God over time, throughout our many life experiences. We often see their growth most clearly after the *difficult* times.

We've observed these qualities in the life of Beth Raney. In 1968 Beth and her husband, George, were missionaries in the Philippines. With three small children and another child on the way, their work on the underdeveloped island of Palawan wasn't easy. But Beth said that she and George felt they were experiencing a dream come true—a dream to bring good news to people who hadn't heard there is a God who loves them.

Dreams, however, don't always have happy endings. Here's the story in Beth's words. "In the late afternoon, on December 22, 1968, I was standing by on our air-to-ground radio expecting my pilot husband to report 'drop complete.' Instead I heard the jumbled garble of our point-to-point radio. I switched over to hear, 'Beth, George's plane has had an engine failure and was last seen gliding over the trees.' Although he had successfully spiraled down to drop the supplies needed for the missionaries in Tabon, there was no place to land the plane except mountains and trees. In a matter of seconds, George was in the presence of the Lord he deeply loved."

Beth continued, "It made no logical sense. My loving husband and the devoted father of our children was gone. It was as if God had allowed both of my legs to be cut off. As in an amputation, the pain was beyond description. I could only hold on to the God who had loved me and called me to himself. There were times I felt like I was hanging onto a window ledge twelve stories high with only my fingernails. Other times it seemed like huge ocean waves would come and sweep me off my feet and tumble me about so I did not know which way was up and I wondered if I would survive. Many times I cried out to God asking him for strength, wisdom and the ability to persevere."

Two years after George's death, Beth chose to return to the Philippines with her four children and hold Bible clubs for children there, because God's plans for her had not stopped. As a confident woman, she knew she had a calling and a ministry of her own. Her mission then asked her to meet a critical need for a nurse at its international school in Indonesia. In God's providence, this was a wonderful answer to her prayers, because in Indonesia God brought men who were good role models into the lives of her sons. The head mechanic at the mission airport took her boys under his wing, letting them help in the airplane hangar and wash airplanes. As they grew older, the boys even learned how to work on engines.

It is not surprising to anyone who knows Beth that all four of her children and their spouses are now serving God in various countries around the world. Her children have also faced their own sufferings, but they have the wonderful example of a mom who confidently trusted and continues to trust God.

Beth says, "The difficult circumstances in my life prompted me to ask two questions: Is God really good? Is God really enough? Those questions were answered for me as I found my identity in Christ. I like to think of my identity in Christ as two sides of the same coin. On one side, I discovered who God is, and on the other side, I discovered who I am because of who God is. As I've studied the life of Christ in the Bible, observing how Christ related to his Father and to the people around him, I have grown in confidence as I have learned about the character of God and have experienced it myself."

> *Our society today bears all the marks of a God-starved community. Where there is no belief in a purpose extending beyond this life, people are inevitably oppressed by a sense of futility.*
> J. B. PHILLIPS

Confidence Reaches Out

Since a Christ-follower's goal in life is not personal fulfillment at any cost, confidence is not an end in itself. Rather, the confidence we gain because of our identity as God's dearly loved children empowers us to live beyond ourselves, reaching out to others as God desires for us to do.

The more we claim our identity as confident children of God, the more we become responsible, mature adults whose purpose is to reflect God to those around us. With God's help, we begin to find more confidence to go around—not just for our sake but for the sake of others as well.

Reflection Questions

1. How does being a child of God affect your identity?

2. What was one confidence-building experience in your life?

3. Read Exodus 3:7—4:5. How did God respond to Moses' confidence crisis?

4. Read 2 Kings 4:1-7. How did Elisha respond to the widow's needs? What do you suppose this did for her confidence?

5. Read Psalm 36. How does a life of faith in God promote confidence? How does a life of rebellion against God undermine confidence?

6. What is one tradition from your family of origin that influenced your level of confidence?

7. What is one faulty belief that you have struggled with?

8. How would you describe yourself to a new acquaintance? What is your personal style?

4

It's About Time! Finding More of It

Teach us to number our days aright,
that we may gain a heart of wisdom.

PSALM 90:12

One afternoon, a dad returned home from work and found his house in total chaos. His three children were outside playing in the mud, still in their pajamas at 5:30 p.m. Empty food boxes and wrappers were strewn all over the front yard. The door of his wife's car was open, as was the front door to their house.

Proceeding into the house, he found an even bigger mess. Someone had knocked over a lamp, and a throw rug was wadded up against one wall. In the front room the TV was blaring, and the family room was cluttered with toys and clothing. In the kitchen, dishes filled the sink, breakfast food was spilled on the counter, and a broken glass lay under the table.

Looking for his wife, the man bounded up the stairs, stepping over toys and more piles of clothing. He was worried that his wife was ill or that something serious had happened.

He found his wife. She was lounging in the bedroom—still in her pajamas, reading a novel. Looking up at her husband, she smiled and asked how his day went.

Bewildered, the man asked, "What's going on?"

His wife answered, "You know every day when you come home from work and ask, 'What in the world did you do today?'"

"Yes," her husband responded.

"Well," she said, "today I didn't do it."

We chuckle at this story because we sometimes feel that we don't have much to show for a full day's work. Although the story is fiction, the feeling of *I didn't accomplish enough* is distinctly real. In our more serious moments we think about the big picture and wonder, *What am I accomplishing? Am I headed in the right direction? At the end of my life, will I have enough to show for all of my busy days?*

> *Jesus never seemed to hurry anywhere, yet we are told that he finished every single one of his objectives during his short life. The night before his agony on the cross began and his earthly life ended, he looked toward heaven and prayed, "I have brought you glory on earth by completing the work you gave me to do" (John 17:4). And as he drew his last breath, he made the incredible statement, "It is finished" (John 19:30). Nothing essential was left undone.*
> CHARLES BRADSHAW
> AND DAVE GILBERT

Only one man in the history of the earth managed his life perfectly, and his life spanned a mere thirty-three years. Jesus managed his life according to what was most important and accomplished all the work God gave him to do. In the Bible we see some of Jesus' priorities: pointing us to God, showing us God's truth and grace, rescuing us from sin and praying for us—which he still does!

All these priorities involved people and their relationship to God; Jesus left us a powerful example of what is most important. The only way we will have enough time, energy or resources to accomplish all that *we* need to accomplish is to look to God for strength and manage *our* lives according to what is most important. As we seek God's wisdom, what is most important to him becomes important to us.

> *There is always enough time in any one day to do the things Christ wants us to do. He has called us to be faithful, not frantic.*
> LLOYD JOHN OGILVIE

A few years ago I (Ellen) read a book that encouraged me to create a personal mission statement. I'd read books like that before, but I'd always skipped over the part about writing a mission statement. This time, though, I *had* to do it. I was leading a group of friends in a study on that particular chapter of the book.

After thinking about my priorities and putting a mission statement on paper (one paragraph), I wished that I had done it sooner. I began praying the sentences of my mission statement each day, and this habit continues to help me in several ways. First, I'm reminded daily that I need God's help. Second, I focus on the most important things as I'm praying about them. Third, I'm making progress in saying no to things that would distract me from the most important things. Knowing what's most important in life and ordering my days accordingly is what helps me manage my resources well. When I *don't* think about what's most important and plan around that, it feels as though everything and everyone else is arranging my life.

Once we've established what's most important, we're ready to look at how we manage our time. Although God is infinite and is not limited by time, we are. We all live with time constraints. We're constantly trying to push our limits (just look in the *Guinness Book of World Records*), but limits will always be part of our lives. Since life is short, let's investigate some of the ways we can use time wisely.

Tips to Help Manage Time — A Baker's Dozen

1. *Do the most important thing first.* Some years ago, Charles Schwab sent Ivy Lee a twenty-five-thousand-dollar check for *one* time-management tip. According to Schwab, it was the most profitable tip he had received in his long business career. Here it is: Think about the most important things that you need to do tomorrow. Write them down, and number each task according to its importance. Tomorrow morning, begin task number one and stay with it until it's completed. Keep going down the list. Don't worry if you don't complete everything by the end of the day; at least you will have completed the most important projects. *Do this every day.*

Following this tip helps us avoid flitting from one thing to another or beginning a bunch of projects without completing them.

As I (Ellen) am working on this paragraph, I'm thinking about *my* day. The first two things on my list I've already accomplished—devotional time and an outside walk. I'm presently working on number three—several hours of work on this book. Numbers four, five and six are picking up a few things at the grocery store, preparing dinner for tonight's company and sorting through a messy pile of papers on my kitchen desk. Number six can wait until tomorrow if it has to—it's likely that it will—but numbers four and five must be accomplished today.

Because I (Joan) enjoy crossing things off lists, I have been known to write things on a list *after* I've done them so I could have the satisfaction of seeing how much I accomplished. This is especially helpful on days when I felt I was just spinning my wheels.

2. *Don't put it off.* Worrying about tasks that didn't get completed often causes us more stress than actually doing the task. From our own experiences in procrastination, we offer you a tip that helps us avoid putting important things off. If you're overwhelmed, try the "Swiss cheese method." Developed by Alan Lakein, a time management expert, this method cuts the cheese (the job) into small pieces. If you break down a job into small parts, you may have an easier time getting started. Do *something*—it will get your enthusiasm going.

> *Don't put off for tomorrow what you can do today, because if you enjoy it today you can do it again tomorrow.*
> JAMES MICHENER

When we began writing this chapter, the task seemed overwhelming until we organized our outline and began working on small sections. Now we are sailing along and we won't feel overwhelmed again—until we begin the next chapter.

In The Family Manager *Kathy Peel offers seven wonderful tips on how to get out from under the pile when we've procrastinated.*

1. Set a date and time very soon to tackle an unpleasant task. Write it on your calendar.

2. If it's a big task you're dreading, do it in little pieces. [There's that Swiss cheese idea again.]

3. Tell a friend that you have to accomplish your distasteful task by a certain time. The task itself seems better than facing embarrassment.

4. Delegate the task to someone else.

5. If you feel overwhelmed by a task that seems too complex, treat it like a jigsaw puzzle and work on the "edges" of the problem.

6. If a task is hard to do for emotional rather than technical reasons—for example, you need to talk to a neighbor about her child's misbehavior—remember that you're only going to feel worse the longer the task hangs over your head.

7. Sometimes we procrastinate about making a decision because we want desperately to be right. In this case it's fear that's holding us back. But the fact is, by procrastinating we are actually making a decision—a decision not to act at all.

KATHY PEEL, The Family Manager *(Dallas: Word, 1996), pp. 102-4.*

When I (Joan) was adjusting to being an at-home mom with toddlers, after having worked to put Jim through medical school, I discovered the need for intentional structure in my days. Having observed young moms in our apartment complex who were still in hair rollers and bathrobes at noon, I secretly devised "the 9:00 a.m. rule" for myself. My rule meant that by 9:00 the kids and I were dressed, the beds were made, breakfast dishes were done, and we were ready to meet the day. It was satisfying to consolidate several repetitive tasks into one small part of my morning, so that they didn't consume my entire day.

3. *Plan ahead.* Plan monthly. If your calendar is like ours, it fills up quickly. Sometimes we'll flip to a new month and think, *Wow! How did the second week of this month get packed so tight?* If that's the case, put a halt to scheduling anything more, or shift a few things around to a different week. It's no fun to dread a month before it even begins.

At the beginning of each month, I (Joan) take my calendar and birthday book to a card shop and choose greeting cards for all the birthdays and special events falling in that month. When I get home, I write on each envelope (in very small numbers underneath the spot for the stamp) the date I need to mail the card; then I arrange the cards in a folder chronologically. Planning ahead saves me time.

Another way to plan monthly is to join, or start, a cooking co-op. We know three young moms who have done this. Once a month each woman cooks three family-size portions of a favorite recipe, such as lasagna, meatloaf or chicken and dumplings, which they freeze and swap. They have eliminated the confusion of dish returns by using color-coded dishes. Jan cooks in white Corning, Jackie uses clear Pyrex, and Dawn has amber Pyrex. Each woman spends one morning a month doing some "marathon" cooking but then has three delicious meals waiting in the freezer for busy days when there just isn't enough time to go around.

Plan weekly. Before the beginning of each new week, sit down to think about *big rocks*. When popular author and speaker Stephen Covey presents his First Things First seminars, he frequently demonstrates the principle of important things with three small containers and one large-mouth jar. The first container holds big rocks, the second container holds gravel, and the third container holds sand. The large-mouth jar is empty.

Participants of the seminar are asked to fit as much of the contents of the three containers as possible into the large-mouth jar. Those who get the most contents in are people who begin with the big rocks, add gravel and then pour in sand to fill the empty spaces. If participants put sand and gravel in first, there's no room left for the big rocks.

Our lives operate on a similar principle. If we fill up our days with myriad busy things (sand and gravel), we won't have any space left for the most *important* things (big rocks). Plan for the big rocks first.

"Adjoinings of time" are what I (Joan) call those valuable snatches of time in between the scheduled events of the day (big rocks). They can be utilized creatively. To be prepared for these unexpected moments, I keep a book, notepaper and extra walking shoes in my car. Sometimes I'm pleasantly surprised with opportunities to read, write or take a walk in the middle of my day.

Plan daily. Write out a schedule for each day, preferably at the beginning of each week. After you've recorded your fixed appointments, write down things you need to do and other things you'd *like* to do. Work on the most important things first. The other things will fall into place. Spend five minutes each morning with your coffee cup and day planner, collecting your thoughts and getting a sense of where your day's headed.

Don't forget to look at your calendar *every* day. We state the obvious because I (Ellen) recently forgot to *do* the obvious. One of the mornings that I was working on *this chapter,* I forgot to check my calendar. I didn't remember until late that afternoon that I was supposed to have introduced a speaker at a professional meeting earlier in the morning. First I panicked, next I felt awful, and finally I settled down and reminded myself that no one is perfect. I apologized to the people involved and realized again *my* need to check the calendar daily.

Since our daily, weekly and monthly activities are strong indicators of what we think is most important, we are wise to ask—regularly—*Am I pleased with the balance?* Prioritizing our life becomes an intentional endeavor, so we are not waking up to realize that we've said yes to much too much and are living a helter-skelter existence.

4. *Organize your space.* We asked our friend Ruthie, who is one of the most organized people we know, "What's the best way to organize any space?"

She gave us three pointers. (1) Get rid of anything you don't use (unless it's a priceless heirloom). The less you own, the less time it takes to care for what you own. (2) Assign a place for everything. (3) Use the space you've assigned.

Are you a packrat or a "thrower-outer"? Often there's one of each in a household, and it produces some interesting family dynamics. I (Joan) believe that the frequent geographical relocations of my childhood and youth contributed to my semi-conscious thought *I'll move again so I'd better not accumulate*—hence I love to pitch things I'm no longer using. When things in our home can't be found, guess who is the immediate suspect!

When our family moved from our home of twenty-five years into a lower-maintenance "empty nest" home, my sister-in-law Carla volunteered to help pack. Not having emotional ties to our stuff, she found it easy to pitch a lot. Now if things are missing the blame falls on her, with the oft-heard comment, "Carla probably pitched it." It's not a bad idea to enlist the help of a neutral helper if we really want to minimize clutter. It's amazing what we can live without.

My mother, who lost many of her earthly belongings in various evacuations in China, was often heard to say, "Blessed is nothing." In her later years she told our family, "If I can't eat it or wear it, I don't want it." In other words, she didn't want anymore bric-a-brac. When she died in 1990, she left very little behind because she didn't need stuff to make her happy. She loved giving away what she did have, and she received great joy in giving her few cut-glass pieces to me, her cloisonné to my sister Carol, and her ivory to my brother Bob before she died. Now we each have a *few* of her choice mementos to pass on to our children—along with her wonderful, more lasting legacies of faith in God, love for her family and wonderful sense of humor. Oh yes, there are also memories of her incredible homemade cinnamon rolls, which two of her granddaughters have learned to replicate.

My mother's example inspires me as I clear out clutter. One of my methods is to keep a giveaway closet in our guestroom. If I find clothes that I haven't worn in a couple of years, I put them into this closet, from which guests (many of whom are missionaries or internationals) are invited to help themselves. One missionary friend says that upon arriving in the United States from Indonesia, she makes a beeline from O'Hare International Airport to our home to replenish her wardrobe before she appears anywhere in public. Even if the clothes still fit me,

I figure that if I haven't worn them in the last two years I don't really need them anymore.

Garage sales are also a great way to clear out excess on a regular basis—as long as we aren't stopping at other sales to reaccumulate what we've just eliminated. Constantly recycling stuff without any bottom-line losses becomes a problem. A policy of stopping at garage sales only to look for one or two specific needed items might help. The same could be said for the attraction of discount-store shopping. We probably haven't saved any money or reduced our accumulated volume of things if we bought something because it was "such a great price." Stop to ask yourself if you'd buy this item even if it weren't on sale.

The benefit in reducing clutter is that it enables us to live less encumbered lives. Reducing the clutter of "stuff" provides more time and energy for what's important.

5. *Delegate.* Many times we assume that it's too difficult to explain tasks or responsibilities to anyone else, so we attempt to do everything ourselves. Not being able to delegate may also reflect a need to ensure a "perfect" outcome every time— another indication of our perfectionism. If this is the way we approach our family, church responsibilities or job, there will never be enough of us to go around. The dictionary defines *delegating* as trusting something to another person. Delegating— when done with respect and not because we're lazy—can be affirming to the people we live with and work with.

Delegating begins early with young children when we say, "Please finish picking up your cars by the time the song on your tape is done." The good news is that older children are capable of performing bigger jobs. One Friday evening when I (Ellen) was preparing for out-of town-guests, everything in our house seemed to break loose. Because I knew there wasn't enough time to go around to put clean sheets on beds and also shop at the grocery store, I asked my high school son, Nate, and his buddy Mark if they would take my grocery list and do the shopping. The guys agreed, and they had fun in the process. I wished I could have been a fly on the wall in the grocery store. Returning to the house laughing and joking, Nate and Mark even put things away. I did end up with a few surprises in my pantry.

For years I (Joan) had an SVP (*s'il vous plaît*) list on my fridge that included things I hoped Jim would do around the house. When he had the time and energy, he'd look at my list, and things got done without any nagging. Some women call this their "honey-do" list.

If you're ever feeling overwhelmed about home, church or work, take out a piece of paper and write down any job that could be accomplished by another family member or coworker. You're already halfway there when you've identified someone who could do the job. The other half is to ask for your family member or coworker's help—carefully and respectfully. Delegating helps us find time for the most important things.

6. *Learn how to say no.* I (Ellen) recently received an invitation to speak at a college music workshop. Although I wanted to accept, the event fell at a time of year when my family was already very busy, so I declined. Saying no was hard, but if I had accepted, I would have felt frustrated when the weekend of the event rolled around, and I wouldn't have had enough time for the most important things in my life.

A subtle method of saying no is to ask oneself, *What can I leave off?* Leaving something off our list instantly expands our time. One morning when I (Ellen) was working on this chapter, I was looking forward to having friends come for dinner in the evening. In order to increase my writing time, I made a quick decision to serve ice-cream sundaes for dessert instead of baking the chocolate cake I had originally envisioned. This little decision expanded my writing time by thirty minutes, and for that day writing was more important than baking.

Sometimes we need to remember that we can give ourselves permission to serve ice cream instead of a fancy dessert. When it comes to desserts, I (Joan) often say, "Anything I can do, Sara Lee can do better." Small no's add time and decrease stress. Eliminating activities that don't mesh with our life purpose or mission statement presents us with more time to do the most important things.

I can provide a simple prescription for a happier, healthier life, but it must be implemented by the individual family. You must resolve to slow your pace; you must learn to say "no" gracefully; you must resist the temptation to chase after more pleasures, more hobbies, more social entanglements; you must "hold the line" with the tenacity of a tackle for a professional football team, blocking out the intruders and defending the home team. In essence, three questions should be asked about every new activity that presents itself: Is it worthy of our time? What will be eliminated if it is added? What will be its impact on our family life? My suspicion is that most of the items in our busy day would score rather poorly on this three-item test.
JAMES DOBSON, Prescription for a Tired Homemaker (Wheaton, Ill.: Tyndale House, 1987), p. 18.

---

7. *Deal with interruptions.* As much as we'd like to get rid of them, we need to realize that there will *always* be interruptions, so it's realistic to allow for a few each day. We don't want to feel that our lives are thrown into turmoil when we adjust our schedules to place relationships ahead of tasks. One of our friends, Gretchen, prays each morning about the interruptions she assumes will happen in her day. She has learned that in God's providence, interruptions sometimes become divine appointments.

If interruptions get out of control, though, we won't be able to accomplish the most important things. The business executive may be able to hang a "Please do not disturb" sign on her office door, but how can those of us who are homemakers control interruptions? We need to have enough respect for ourselves to realize that the business executive's days and tasks are no more important than the homemaker's. Then we can stand back, take a look at our day and ask, "Are there measures I can take to *avoid* interruptions at various parts of my day?"

A young mom might hire a babysitter to play with her children while she spends an afternoon working on a project or goes shopping. Some moms of young children establish a "quiet hour" or "book rest" after lunch (or whenever it works well), when the children must stay in their rooms and play quietly or read. Preschool children need an opportunity to rest in the middle of their energetic days—and their moms need to recharge their batteries before the infamous dinner hour. Launching this plan may be a challenge, but the peace and quiet it brings feels like a lifeline for young moms.

Be creative! You'll come up with methods that are appropriate for your schedule, and even if you eliminate only a few interruptions, you'll have more time to devote to important things.

8. *Communicate clearly.* When you're headed out to pick up a replacement part for your oven, don't leave your house

Reliable communication permits progress.
PROVERBS 13:17 (LB)

until you've called ahead to confirm that the part is in stock. Calling ahead saves precious minutes. "Let your fingers do the walking" is good advice from the publishers of the Yellow Pages.

When you're dealing with plans made between children, it doesn't hurt to clarify details *twice.* As much as we want our children to learn independence on the telephone, we are wise to clarify directions on how to get to a friend's house at 123 West Oak Street. Otherwise we may find ourselves driving down *East* Oak Street and discovering that no such house number exists. This scenario happened several times to me (Ellen), prompting Jim and me to begin speaking person to person with other parents when directions were involved. Part of communicating clearly is attempting to identify potential problems *ahead* of time.

9. *Limit paperwork.* Heeding advice to handle papers only once has helped me (Ellen) in the process of managing paperwork. Purchasing and organizing a pretty filing basket in my kitchen has taken *some* of the clutter off my kitchen counters. I've labeled files for each child, files for menu plans, files for upcoming events—basically I have files for everything in my life.

My (Joan) niece Sarah has a wonderful solution for papers that threaten to clutter her kitchen counter. She purchased a large three-ring binder and clear 8x11 envelope sheets to go in it—about twenty or thirty. They're a little like big photo-album pages, except that this binder contains all the stuff that often accumulates on counters, desks or telephone cabinets. In the first clear envelope page, she inserts her typed telephone list of airlines, auto care, bakery, bookstores, carry-out restaurants, church, florists, grocery stores and so on. In the second clear page, she inserts a page of emergency numbers. Other pages contain neighborhood phone numbers, family birthdays and anniversaries, school calendars, group lists (Bible studies, soccer teams, tennis teams), Christmas wish lists; there's even a page for everyone's social security number. It's also a great place to store invitations or RSVP cards. *Warning!* All of your family members will enjoy using such a notebook as much as you do. Consider chaining it to your desk.

Color-coding pages on the family calendar to denote certain jobs or activities for each family member is helpful. Each child is responsible to look for his or her color. Sarah's daughter Caroline says, "I just look for what's written in pink because that means *me*." Parents who are sharing custody find this is a good way to quickly identify their days or weekends and avoid schedule conflicts. We can also highlight days we are scheduled to take refreshments to a school or church function—it's so embarrassing to forget.

10. *Make lists.* Lists are records that help us keep our life running smoothly. Although any woman's lists may include accounts, agendas, inventories and schedules, here we will address three lists: the weekly menu, the shopping list and the food preparation list. Do you notice that food is the common denominator?

Probably the most obvious reason for planning a *weekly menu* (or a monthly menu if we're ambitious) is that we won't have to decide daily what to make for dinner each night. We only need to figure out our menu once a week, and the rest of the days we work our plan. Another good reason for planning a menu is that we save money, because we're not running to the grocery store every day. I (Ellen) have had weeks when, as a result of my lack of planning, I showed up at the grocery store five days in a row. Grocery stores love people like me. Planning a weekly menu, however, saves us time and money.

Extra hint: Take inventory of what's in your refrigerator and pantry before making up your menu. I (Ellen) recently discovered that I had an abundance of chocolate chips, canned pumpkin and cream cheese. Amazingly, I came across a recipe for pumpkin chocolate-chip cookies with chocolate cream cheese icing. The cookies were great and so was the feeling of using what I had.

Have you ever lost a *grocery list?* Trying to reconstruct it in your head is no easy task, unless your original list was very short. Grocery lists help us avoid running back to the store and—if organized well—help us avoid running back and forth within the store. Ideally we should have a grocery list going all the time, tucked in our wallet or posted on the refrigerator door. When we're getting low on sugar, flour or other necessities, we can add them to the list.

Another ideal is to plan menus and shopping lists when we know what's on sale at our favorite grocery store. I (Ellen) shop at a small, warehouse-type, bag-your-own-groceries store once a week (while Jordan takes his trumpet lesson), and I buy staple foods at low prices. I've got my routine down, and I can be in and out of there in twenty minutes. Then I purchase meat, produce and family favorites at the neighborhood grocery store.

I (Joan) plan ahead and stock up on necessary ingredients for my favorite meals. I buy chicken breasts for sweet and sour chicken, cottage cheese and sour cream for crustless quiche. I specialize in "thirty-minute quickies" that can be on the table soon after I get home from work.

There's no one approach to grocery shopping that works for everyone, but good planning makes our life easier—we save both time and money.

It makes sense to jot down a *food preparation list* before launching into a major meal. When I (Joan) am preparing a special meal for guests or holiday occasions, I write out the menu—with an approximate timetable for preparation—and tape it to the inside of a kitchen cabinet. If I later get distracted by greeting guests or filling glasses with ice, a glance inside the cabinet helps me to remember what I need to be doing when.

11. *Limit telephone time.* Telephones can be extremely help-

ful. I (Ellen) was grateful for quick access to an ambulance one summer afternoon when my son seriously injured his leg. As I waited (only two minutes) for the ambulance to come, I wondered what moms did without telephones—and orthopedic surgeons—back in prairie days.

As helpful as they are, telephones can also feel like a nuisance. Receiving yet another phone call from a long-winded talker sometimes leaves us feeling that we wasted thirty minutes or more of precious time. The good news is that telephones can be managed with a few simple suggestions.

When placing phone calls, clump them together. For one person 9:00 a.m. may be most convenient, but evening may work best for you.

After you've set aside a chunk of time to make calls, or if you receive a phone call and know you might be on for a while, find another job to accomplish while you're talking or listening. Wiping off kitchen counters, folding a load of laundry and emptying the dishwasher seem to work well. Vacuuming, crushing ice in the blender or typing, however, is not recommended. *Warning!* Consider setting your phone down before removing trays from a hot oven. I (Ellen) once dropped my cordless phone into the bottom of the oven while I was trying to talk and remove cookies at the same time. (Although one side of my phone melted and looks a little funny, it still works.)

When I (Joan) want to catch up on phone calls, I set up my ironing board and double-task. Because earring contact shorts out the phone, I usually remove one earring when I set up the ironing board. If I forget to replace my earring before going out, and I run into someone who knows my habits, they know I've been double-tasking again. I'm hoping to receive a telephone headset for Christmas one of these years.

Finally, if you're calling a friend who speaks seventy-five

thousand words a day (instead of the average twenty-five thousand), you may need to call her five minutes before you leave the house and say, "Hi, I only have five minutes before I leave to take Joanie to viola lessons, but I wanted to touch base with you . . ."

12. *You don't have to stay for the whole meeting.* Unless you're Scottish, that is. We recently heard about a man who sent a postcard to his son that read, "I'm writing you this postcard while I sit in my car in a parking space. I paid for my time, and I'll stay here until the meter expires. Love, Your Scottish Father."

If you're attending a seminar and you discover that there's one meeting in the middle of the day that's not important to you, it's OK to accomplish something else during that hour. Run an errand, return a few phone calls or pray for a hurting friend. And if you've agreed to serve on a committee, it doesn't mean you've agreed to do *all* the work. It's OK to say, "I can't do everything, but I can do *one* thing." It's OK to say, "I need to leave the meeting by 9:00." We just can't do it all, and we need not feel obligated to fall into line with everyone else's goals and agendas.

13. *Get the family working as a team.* While walking outside this morning, I (Ellen) almost stepped on a small yellow leaf. When I observed that the leaf was being carried along by a group of ants, I stopped and watched. Working together, the ants were accomplishing a task much larger than any one ant could have accomplished alone. The ants worked together to carry the yellow leaf across the sidewalk.

Our families can function the same way. Some tasks, like brushing our teeth, are meant to be done alone. Other tasks, like clearing the dinner table or cleaning the house, can be performed more quickly and efficiently if we do them together. If Mom is a busy woman (what mom isn't?), why should she attempt to "carry the leaf" alone? Why do some moms go back to work to put kids through college but hesitate to ask other family members to pitch in around the house?

In my (Ellen's) family, housecleaning has been accomplished in different ways at different times. When the children were young, I did all of the cleaning myself—here a little, there a little. As the children grew and I became more involved in their activities as well as my music and writing projects, the whole family cleaned together. The girls who marry my sons will indeed be lucky women, because my sons know how to clean. (This may not be apparent in a look at their bedrooms, however.) When all the kids were still living at home, our whole family set aside an hour or two when we all participated, dividing up the tasks of vacuuming, dusting, mopping floors and cleaning bathrooms. Afterward we sometimes celebrated our clean house (I celebrated that it was clean, the kids celebrated that it was *over*) by ordering a pizza or going out for ice cream. Because my youngest son, Jordan, is presently on a quest to earn money, our current cleaning plan involves Jordan doing all the vacuuming, for a fee. I dust, clean the bathrooms and mop the floors, and Jim cleans the showers.

> *Women, for hormonal reasons, can see individual dirt molecules, whereas men tend not to notice them until they join together into clumps large enough to support commercial agriculture.*
> DAVE BARRY

There are many creative ways for families to tackle projects together. Parents end up with more time for important things, and kids learn responsibility while their confidence increases.

Keeping Perspective

Sometimes we groan, moan or roll our eyes when we think of attempting to manage our time effectively. If we've fallen short—who hasn't?—we may feel like throwing our hands up in despair: "It's no use! I can't do it perfectly."

Of *course* we can't do it perfectly, nor can we do it all. That's one of the themes of this book. But as we admit we can't do it all and become intentional about what's most important, we will find more to go around.

Daniel, an Old Testament character, is an example of a person who purposed to live intentionally. When Daniel, as a teenager, was taken from his Jewish home into Babylonian captivity, he chose to hold fast to the most important things. In moments of difficulty he realized his need for help and turned to God. He concentrated on the essentials of giving thanks, praying and being available to God. Daniel 1:8 begins, "But Daniel resolved . . ."

After we ask for God's help, we too need to focus on things that matter the most. Daniel purposed in his heart to do the most important things, and God blessed him and lifted him up. Resolve to do the same, and through small, deliberate choices you can realize big changes in the quality of your life—there *will* be more to go around!

Reflection Questions

1. Read John 17. What things were important to Jesus?

2. Write out your personal mission statement in one short—or long—paragraph.

3. What is one of your biggest time-wasters?

4. What is one area in which you have been learning to say no?

5. What is one thing you have been putting off that you might tackle this week?

6. What is one thing that you might consider delegating to someone else?

7. Read chapters 1 and 6 of Daniel. What was most important to Daniel? What were Daniel's needs? How were his needs met?

5

Help!
We Need Boundaries!

Stay always within the boundaries where
God's love can reach and bless you.

JUDE 21 (LB)

$\mathcal{D}$uring the early years of Bill and Lisa's marriage, lengthy visits from Lisa's parents were dreaded events. Lisa's parents typically called and announced when they would be arriving, and they often ended up staying for several weeks. Even though Lisa and Bill resented the way Lisa's parents descended on them, they went along with the pattern for years. Over those years, relations with Lisa's parents grew worse. But that wasn't the only thing that grew worse. Resentment and tension between Bill and Lisa began to escalate as well.

After one especially difficult visit they decided to seek the help of a counselor. As a result of spending time identifying problems and negotiating some constructive changes, Lisa and

Bill decided that it was time to set some boundaries.

The next time Lisa's parents called and announced that they were coming for two weeks, Bill and Lisa said, "Mom and Dad, we need to talk about visits. We've decided that two weeks is just too long for us to have houseguests. A five-day visit would be more workable for us, so let's decide which five days will work for all of us."

> A boundary is a limit
> that promotes integrity.
> ANNE KATHERINE

This approach took Lisa's parents by surprise, and they weren't particularly pleased by the idea, but Lisa and Bill gently but firmly stood their ground. When Lisa's parents realized that their daughter and son-in-law were serious and that they were operating as a team (*very* important), they eventually accepted the idea of a five-day visit.

When Lisa's parents did arrive, Bill and Lisa noticed that Lisa's parents treated them both with a little more respect than before. The young couple agreed that although setting a boundary had required careful thought and lots of courage, the positive results were well worth their efforts.

If you are wondering whether setting some boundaries might help to improve the quality of your life, you're not alone. Many of us find boundary issues to be a huge challenge. We may realize that we need to draw boundaries when

☐ we're disappointed with our own choices

☐ we have a hard time saying no—somehow we think that we should do it all

☐ we feel as if we're at the mercy of a family member whose behavior is causing us a lot of difficulty or pain

☐ our children seem to be controlling us

☐ someone is treating us inappropriately

As we walk around our neighborhood, we can usually identify which homeowners have installed invisible fences. Dogs may start bounding across the lawn, but they've learned not to cross a particular line, lest they receive a small but uncomfortable shock.

Like buried electronic pet fences around the perimeter of a yard, boundaries can help us avoid threatening circumstances or relationships. Dogs aren't the only ones who need boundaries. People need them too. We only wish that establishing boundaries were as simple as installing an electronic fence.

Learning to set and respect healthy boundaries involves taking responsibility for our body, feelings, thoughts, behaviors, desires and limits. In all these areas the challenge, according to authors Henry Cloud and John Townsend, is knowing when to say yes and when to say no. If we continually say yes to everything that comes our way, not only will we run into all kinds of trouble, but we'll never have enough to go around.

As we accept the identity God has given us and learn what we will say yes to and no to, we'll begin to live a healthier life and find that there's more to go around. In looking at some of the ways our lives are most commonly affected by boundary questions, you may be surprised to discover how much the Bible has to say about the subject.

God's Boundaries Are Gifts

God's Word abounds in narratives that demonstrate what God has said yes to and what he has said no to. In the biblical accounts, people who honor God's boundaries are blessed, and those who don't experience painful consequences. Take Shiprah and Puah, two Hebrew midwives during the Hebrews' period of slavery in Egypt. Although Pharaoh had instructed the midwives to kill all Hebrew baby boys at birth, the Bible records that these midwives feared God and did not do what the king of Egypt told them to do; they let the boys live (Exodus 1:17). Because the midwives honored God's boundary, God blessed them with families of their own. Pharaoh, however, defied God's boundaries and discovered that things in his life did not go so well. In a twist of irony, this selfish king who wanted to drown Hebrew babies in the river ended up watching his huge army drown in the Red Sea (Exodus 15:4-5).

Adam and Eve are the first people in the Bible to feel the consequences of crossing over God's boundaries. God had given them freedom to enjoy all the trees in the Garden of Eden except one. But instead of being grateful for the wide scope of God's goodness, the couple chose to focus on the one restriction God had given them—a behavior that's been common to the human race ever since. When Eve and Adam treated themselves to the fruit of one forbidden tree, they learned that they had to live with the consequences, some of which were loss of innocence, separation from God and death. They learned the truth that people of all generations learn: we can choose our sins, but we can't choose the consequences. What Adam and Eve experienced in the garden we are still experiencing today.

Jenny wishes that she had thought about consequences a little earlier in her life. For years she had been unhappy with her marriage. Although she and her husband had sought counseling, the tension and unresolved issues between them continued to escalate. Feeling sorry for herself, Jenny began to respond to the attention of a man in her office who listened to her and affirmed her. She liked his attention—something she felt she hadn't received from her husband in years. One thing led to another, and Jenny eventually found herself involved in a full-blown affair.

After the initial intrigue and excitement of the affair wore off, Jenny was left with a bitter aftermath that included depression, loss of self-respect, sleepless nights, the unrelenting anger of her husband and some bizarre behavior in her children. The only good thing about her despair was that it prompted her to run into the arms of Christ, who offered her forgiveness and hope. That did not take away the painful consequences of her choices, but it did give her hope to keep going during some very dark days. "I now see," said Jenny, "that when God said 'Do not commit adultery' he wasn't withholding something from me. Rather, he was offering me the gift of protection."

If the need to live with the consequences of our choices were the end of the story, we'd all despair, because we've all made some poor choices. But—thanks to God—the Bible gives us hope for our predicament. Through Jesus' death on the cross, he has saved us from the consequence of eternal separation from God and given us a better way to live in the present. As we put our faith in Christ and choose to walk in the light of God's truth, we experience great freedom, security and peace. We begin to realize that God did not give us boundaries to make us miserable. Rather, he gave them to us to protect us, make us wise, give us joy and light, and warn us away from harm (Psalm 19:7-8, 11). God's boundaries are not a punishment. They are there for our protection.

Setting Limits

Although all of us face boundary issues in our choices between right and wrong, this is not the only kind of boundary issue we face. Scarcely a day goes by that we don't need to draw boundaries based on our limitations. If we choose *not* to give of ourselves, we'll miss out on the deepest joy and satisfaction of life. But if we give too much, trying to be all things to all people at all times, we'll find ourselves running on empty. There won't be enough to go around. Although we can't do it all, we can choose to do the most *important* things.

Mark 1:21-37 records that after Jesus spent an entire day teaching in the Capernaum synagogue, he went to stay at the home of Simon and Andrew. While there, he healed Simon's mother-in-law, who was sick with a fever. Then in an amazing display of need, the whole town gathered at the door after sunset, bringing to Jesus people who were sick and demon-possessed.

It's difficult to imagine how exhausted he must have felt when the last person had departed and he went to bed for the night. But the next morning Jesus made a choice that provided time for him to accomplish his priorities. "Very early in the morning, while it was still dark, Jesus got up, left the house and went off to a solitary place, where he prayed" (Mark 1:35). Because spending time in prayer was important to Jesus, he avoided missing out on that priority by finding a time and a place where he would not be interrupted.

When it feels as though our life is dictated by pressures and demands that we did not choose or agreed to only reluctantly, we need to stop and realize that we *do* have the option of making thoughtful and intentional choices. As we establish appropriate boundaries and act on them confidently, we'll feel less frustration that there's not enough of us to go around, and we'll have more energy for the things that are most important.

I (Ellen) recently learned something about these kinds of boundaries when my two older sons came home from college for a weekend and brought along five other college-age friends. Because I didn't discuss breakfast and lunch schedules with everyone when they arrived, each day the students "grazed" from about 9:00 a.m. until 1:00 p.m. This schedule made it difficult for me to accomplish some important tasks of my own; I felt like a captive in my kitchen. Hindsight being as wonderful as it is, when students come to visit now, I announce breakfast and lunch schedules ahead of time. (Those who sleep late can always grab a bowl of Cocoa Puffs.) That way I can be hospitable to my sons' friends while also accomplishing some of the things that are important to me.

Becky received a phone call from a casual acquaintance of one of her sons, asking if he could come to her house and make a presentation of something—with no obligation to buy, of course. Becky and her husband had sat through enough of

Establishing limits is essential in every relationship and is the basis for mutual respect and love.
HENRY CLOUD

these presentations to know that there's always a strong pitch at the end. She knew that if she scheduled the appointment, she and her husband would sit and squirm because they wouldn't want to buy, but they also wouldn't want to hurt the salesperson's feelings. Since they were short on time and money, Becky thought it was more important to say no than to accommodate her son's friend. So Becky said, "Thanks for thinking of us. We don't presently have the time or money to make scheduling this presentation worthwhile for either of us, but we wish you the best."

She was kind to the young man, while she drew a boundary based on what was most important. If she had gone ahead and scheduled the presentation, she would have resented her decision later, as she had so many times in the past.

Becky used to say yes to anything and everything, and then she'd get irritated with other people for making so many demands on her time. She hadn't learned that often "our 'feeling pressured' is our tendency to agree with the pressurer's attitude instead of setting forth our own. We must get in touch with how we are getting hooked into saying yes and not put the blame on the other person."[1] Over time, Becky did learn how to draw limits, and her life became a lot more manageable.

What's My Responsibility? What's Not?

Another boundary challenge is defining what's our responsibility and what's not. Most of us encounter these issues on a daily basis—especially with family or friends who seem to have difficulty respecting our privacy and space. Although it's not our job to go around telling other people how to live, we can determine what will or won't work for us. "Boundaries are not something you 'set on' another person. Boundaries are about yourself."[2] There is no way we can ever change another person's behavior. But we can draw boundaries so that their behavior doesn't drain us. We don't establish boundaries for the sake of other people, although they may be helpful for another person. We establish boundaries because *we* want to act responsibly.

If we believe that part of our responsibility is keeping the people around us happy, we're probably having trouble drawing appropriate boundaries around our feelings. Our responsibility, as Christ-followers, is to make decisions before God based on what is right, not on how others feel about our choices.

Friendship boundaries. Julie is a young mom whose friends often ask her to baby-sit for their children. At first Julie didn't mind helping, but recently she's started resenting her friends' requests, and she's finding it hard to say no. Maybe Julie needs the gracious honesty to say, "I'm feeling a little overwhelmed right now, so it won't work for me to watch your children today." Or perhaps she needs to work out a balanced baby-sitting exchange with other young moms. Several of the young moms in our community coordinate a babysitting co-op, using coupons to indicate available or utilized hours to be traded. A co-op like this might help Julie with boundaries so that she doesn't become overburdened.

Moms with school-aged children sometimes ask, "How can

we open our homes without becoming neighborhood den mothers?" Nonworking moms sometimes feel responsible for all the latchkey kids on the block. Maybe we intend and feel called to serve that way, but if not, we need to figure out how to be a good neighbor without losing our sanity. I (Joan) know a family with a swimming pool who, in addition to requiring that an adult accompany visiting children, have established the policy that it is when their flag is flying that visitors are welcome. Neighborhood folks know that the flag has more than patriotic significance, and this policy has circumvented many telephone calls, requests, regrets and explanations. Another mom I know opens her garage door to indicate when neighborhood children are welcome to come over and play with her children. It *is* possible to be hospitable and draw boundaries at the same time.

Some women avoid hospitality altogether because they think that they need to provide spotless homes and made-from-scratch meals if they are going to put out the welcome mat. My (Joan's) family would rather draw limits around our expectations of perfect hospitality than miss out on enriching experiences of hosting guests from all over the world. I tell my guests they can put their autograph in the dust on our dining-room table—if they promise not to date it! I also ask houseguests, when they depart, to strip the sheets off the beds and leave them on top of the washer, because the sheets will usually be back on the beds—maybe even slept on—by nightfall.

For each of our guests, we provide house keys that are attached to a Lucite picture of our house, so they don't forget who the key belongs to. Friends in Massachusetts who have graciously housed our family have a system of putting guests' names on notes posted to their hallway banister. As guests come in at night, they are asked to remove the note with their name, and the last one locks the door.

If having guests (especially houseguests) seems daunting to you, try simplifying the process with a few boundaries. What's true in the rest of life is also true of hospitality. People are most comfortable when they understand what's their responsibility and what's not.

> In the long run, being able to say no to loved ones is a necessary skill for keeping these important relationships healthy and strong. . . . Managing life's little tensions as they arise protects your heart from accumulated ill will and frees you up to enjoy your relationships more.
>
> PATTI BREITMAN AND CONNIE HATCH

Family boundaries. It's not unusual for married couples—since they've grown up in different contexts—to have different understandings of boundary systems. John and Maggie were given a down payment on a home as a wedding gift from Maggie's parents. Unfortunately, the gift was given with strings attached—a common way of doing things in Maggie's family. Her parents expressed a desire that their children live in close proximity to them.

As you can imagine, this prompted some spirited conversations between Maggie and John. They came to the wise conclusion that they would accept the gift with gratitude but state that they wanted to live close to their places of employment. This was not easy for them to say, nor was it easy for Maggie's parents to accept, but the outcome was good for John and Maggie's marriage. The young couple drew a boundary by refusing to be manipulated into doing something that wasn't their choice. The way they handled the situation sent a message to Maggie's parents, who probably thought twice before they attempted that approach again—at least with John and Maggie.

Just this morning I (Joan) was chatting with a friend on the phone. She mentioned that her son and daughter-in-law had bought a little "starter home" half a mile from her. Because my friend is a doting grandmother, she noted that she would need to have a conversation with her kids before the moving date to clarify boundaries. Annette said, "My husband and I are the kind of parents who love to be involved in our children's lives. But we don't want to be overbearing or imposing on them. Although we'd enjoy dropping in from time to time, we realize that we need to ask our children what they think of that idea."

I (Joan) like to dive in and be helpful when I visit my adult children, who all live in other parts of the country. But I repeatedly ask them to tell me if I'm overstepping my boundaries—and they do!

Marriage boundaries. It's not unusual for one marriage partner to find it difficult to *set* boundaries while the other finds it harder to *respect* boundaries. One of the ways we build trust in marriage is by learning both to set and to respect boundaries. Sometimes we need to set boundaries with a spouse who would seek to control us with guilt, criticism, temper, manipulation or sarcasm. These things may reflect patterns that have been passed down from previous generations, and sometimes they are outward indications of other unresolved issues. However they surface, they sabotage the growth of intimacy in marriage.

Sally found it challenging to set boundaries, while Don found it difficult to respect them. Don had quite a temper, and Sally dreaded the times he displayed it. For the first few years of their marriage, Sally tolerated Don's temper by tiptoeing around, often feeling like she was walking on eggshells. Sometimes when he was angry, she tried to be helpful, but it wasn't unusual for him to get even more irate then. Sally felt as if she couldn't win for losing. One time, when Don was angrier than she'd ever seen him, he walked into their living room and hurled his keys across the room with such force that they gouged a piece of wood out of the dining-room table.

That did it. What if those keys had hit her or one of their children? Without a word, she gathered up their two toddlers and took them to the park for an hour. Angry, sad and fearful, Sally decided during that hour that when she went home she would deliver a stern message to her husband. "I dislike being around you when you don't control your temper," said Sally. "If you choose to act that way again, I'll leave—whether we're at home, in the car or with other people."

Sally was wise to identify what was going on and to realize how harmful Don's behavior was. (This isn't always easy. It often takes awhile for us to see such a pattern developing.) Second, Sally decided to draw a boundary and clarify what she would do if Don acted that way again. Now that she saw what he was doing, she realized that she didn't have to play his game anymore. (This approach works a lot better than arguing, because, as the old saying goes, actions speak much louder than words.) In a concrete way, Sally learned that "we are not at the mercy of our spouse's behavior or problems. Each spouse can act both to avoid being a victim of the other spouse's problems and better yet, to change the marriage relationship itself."[3]

Parenting boundaries. If we don't set boundaries for our children, they're going to have quite a challenge getting around in the world. They'll end up learning life's lessons from someone else, and "someone else" may or may not be a good role model. "Believe it or not," says family therapist Jodi Conway, "a child who is brought up without boundaries is a terrified child. It's a very scary feeling to know that at age five, you are the boss of the house. These children feel like they're out of control. They often have a hard time coping in school, completing work, and dealing with people."[4]

As much as we realize the need to set boundaries for our children, it's not unusual for us to dread the conflict that saying no produces. It's also not unusual to feel guilty for saying no to something a child really wants. These feelings are normal. But it's important to remember that something's probably wrong if you and your child agree about everything. Any good parent finds that sometimes they need to be the bad guy. Although none of us likes walking into a tense situation or knowing that another person is unhappy with us, sometimes it's necessary to say no.

Patti Breitman and Connie Hatch offer the following ten tips for saying no to kids:

1. Be consistent. No means nothing to your child if you say yes five minutes later.

2. Establish a system of consequences. The bottom line is, you can't effectively say no to your child if he believes there are no consequences for misbehavior.

3. Make eye contact. Before you say a word, ensure that you have your child's full attention. Tell. Don't ask. When speaking to your child, watch your voice: Does it go up at the end of a sentence—you know, like this? If so, concentrate on speaking in a confident, decisive tone.

4. Keep explanations simple and age appropriate.

5. Don't be afraid to repeat yourself. If a child persists in arguing, repeat yourself a few times, using essentially the same language. Then let him know the case is closed.

6. Acknowledge feelings—then move on. Be sympathetic to their feelings, but don't dwell on them. The fact is, the two of you are at odds. It's best to recognize that and move on.

7. Don't belittle. For example, saying, "One piece of cake is enough—you can have another piece tomorrow" is an appropriate way to limit dessert. Saying, "You want another piece? I can't believe what a pig you are!" is degrading.

8. Strive for a united front. When one parent says no and the other says yes, nobody wins. It sends your child confusing messages and invites her to manipulate the situation by "dividing and conquering."

9. Expect cooperation.

10. Be a model parent. Kind, respectful children learn from kind, respectful parents.

PATTI BREITMAN AND CONNIE HATCH, How to Say No Without Feeling Guilty (New York: Broadway, 2000), pp. 162-66.

By learning to distinguish essential issues from nonessential issues, we can minimize the number of times we say no and thus increase its impact. When no means no, a great deal of whining and complaining is eliminated, and Mom has a lot more energy to go around.

Parenting boundaries with adult children. One of the boundary questions that parents of adult children face is, once they've left home, what do we do if they want to move back in?

As the nest is emptying, parents are often caught between feelings of grief and relief. Before they can move on to the next stage of their lives, though, their young adults may want or need to reclaim both living space and privileges. This seems to be occurring more frequently because of educational debts, later marriages and emotional traumas. In *Parenting Your Adult Child* Ross Campbell and Gary Chapman differentiate between the "planners" (children who return briefly as they move on with their life) and the "strugglers" (children who return because they're desperate, often becoming more dependent). Boundaries tend to become more of a challenge with the struggler.

Marty and Ted were happy to provide temporary housing for their daughter, Lindsay, after her company downsized and she was left unemployed. As weeks turned into months, though, Lindsay's "temporary" living arrangement began to feel like it was becoming permanent. Marty and Ted regretted that they hadn't talked to Lindsay early on regarding how long she'd stay, how much rent she'd pay and what her responsibilities would be. After six months, Ted and Marty were experiencing enormous tension over how to handle the situation.

The first—and most important—thing they worked on was coming to an agreement as a couple. Marty and Ted couldn't possibly establish boundaries with Lindsay if they didn't first create a united front between the two of them. That took awhile. But they eventually agreed that they wanted to encourage Lindsay to become a planner, not a struggler.

Ted and Marty knew that they couldn't force their daughter to find a new job or apartment, but they could set limits regarding what would or wouldn't work for them in their home. Consequently they established some boundaries regarding monthly rent and responsibilities, and they specified that Lindsay needed to find her own housing by a date several months down the road. This was difficult for the two parents, but it was necessary for the health of their marriage. In the long run, Marty and Ted discovered that the boundaries they set were helpful not only for their marriage, but they were also helpful for Lindsay. Presented with a deadline, Lindsay gained incentive to find both a new job and an apartment.

Physical Boundaries

When I (Ellen) was a student resident assistant at a Christian college, I was naive about some of the painful situations that students on my floor had already encountered. I'll never forget the night one girl came to my room and told me how her father had sexually abused her during childhood. At the time my brain didn't have a compartment for that type of information.

But the older I've grown, the more of those stories I've heard. Some of the physical boundary violations that cause immense damage in women's lives are incest, abuse and date rape. "Anyone whose body has been violated," says Henry Cloud, "has had his or her personal boundaries horribly injured."[5] Although we can't turn the clock back to protect any woman who experienced such violation in the past, we can be wise about setting physical boundaries ourselves. How can we do this in ways that will be heard and respected?

1. Avoid threatening situations in the first place. If you sense you're in a threatening situation, get out of it immediately. Maybe this advice sounds obvious, but it's something a lot of women overlook.

2. This is not a time for politeness. Be blunt. In a firm voice, say things like "Don't" and "This isn't appropriate" and "How dare you? Don't ever do that again."

3. If a female's no isn't heard—whether she is a child or an adult—she *must* go to a third party to get help (a parent, teacher, pastor, counselor or human relations worker).

Adult women need to be reminded, and young women need to be taught, that when it comes to physical boundaries, each of us has a "forward gear" and a "reverse gear." If someone invades our personal zone, we must use our reverse gear to back away from that person.[6] Any touch that hurts us, harms us or degrades us is violating a boundary. And we can deny it with confidence and without guilt. We all have the right to say no.

Where Do I Begin?

We hope that you have seen how learning when to say yes and when to say no can help you find more to go around. But you may also be thinking, *I've never been good at boundaries. Where do I begin?* Here are a few basic helps to get you going.

Become aware of who you are. Give some thought to your feelings, your attitudes, your behaviors, your choices, your values and your limits. If your husband asks where you'd like to go for your anniversary, don't say, "I don't care." Be honest with yourself and with him about what you'd like to do. "The little Italian café would be great." Or, "How about Chinese?"

Become aware of who you're not. What are some things you don't like, ideas you don't agree with, places you won't go or activities you won't be involved in? If someone suggests a movie that you'd rather not see, say, "That's not a movie I'm comfortable with. How about plan B?"

Avoid the habit of blaming others. Instead decide to do something about life's unfair moments. If your neighbor borrowed your lawn rake and broke it (and it's the third time she's either broken or forgotten to return an item), kindly ask her to replace it or decide that you'll never loan her anything again. As Robert Frost said, "Good fences make good neighbors."

Act, don't react. Some people, especially passive people, spend more energy *reacting* to people around them than *acting* on what they ought to be doing. Some women find it easier to sit home and complain about how they never get a night out with their friends than to actually plan a night out with their friends.

Quit acting like a victim. If you are employed part time in a job where you're miserable, start looking for a new job. You are an adult, you're not stuck, and you can make healthy choices. Women who decide to quit acting like victims and take responsibility for making better choices are amazed at how the quality of their life improves.

Boundaries Require Confidence

Once our antennae are up, we begin to realize that boundary issues have a lot to do with the anxieties each of us faces on a daily basis. Boundaries are tools that help us in managing family issues, moral issues, our own limitations, situations in the corporate world, our property and other people's requests for help. Learning to establish them is an important part of developing a healthy, resilient personality, and it's also one of the ways we can find more to go around.

One boundary issue that I (Ellen) wrestled with involved one of my piano students. By the end of my lessons with Mitch (not his real name), my blood pressure had usually gone up a few notches. Mitch was bright, charming and . . . knew how to push the limits. There always seemed to be a reason he didn't cooperate. He didn't like the way I counted. He didn't like my piano lamp. He didn't like the way I pointed at the music. One day, in the middle of a lesson, Mitch jumped off the piano bench, ran to the other side of the room and wouldn't come back. I tried to coax him back. His father tried to coax him back. But Mitch just stood there, moaning.

I had reached my limit. I handed the music to Mitch's father, looked at them both and said, "The lesson's over."

When Mitch realized what had happened, he ran outside my house and stood in the driveway, crying. His father, with sincerity, said "Thank you" to me as he walked out the door to collect Mitch.

Later that evening, I called the parents and explained that if that ever happened again, they would need to find a new teacher. I'm pleased to say that it didn't happen again. As I look back on that situation now, the only thing I regret is that I didn't draw a boundary sooner.

What boundary challenge is causing *you* anxiety today? Is it a family issue? A job issue? A neighborhood issue? Boundary issues that aren't dealt with may deplete you of energy that you can't afford to lose. But if you work to identify and maintain appropriate boundaries, it's likely that you'll find more to go around. You may even wonder why you hadn't considered them sooner.

Reflection Questions

1. Think of one boundary issue from the past that was challenging for you. How did you deal with it? What was the outcome?

2. Read Exodus 1:1-22; 5:1—6:27; 14:1-31. What boundaries do you observe? How were they followed or violated? What were the results or consequences?

3. Read Genesis 2:15-24; 3:1-24. What boundaries do you observe? How did Adam and Eve observe or cross God's boundaries? What were their excuses? What were the consequences?

4. Read Mark 1:21-39. What boundaries do you see here?

5. What, in your opinion, is one reason it is difficult for us to set limits or say no?

6

Families—Are They Making or Breaking Us?

The LORD is good and his love endures forever;
his faithfulness continues through all generations.

PSALM 100:5

An elderly man in Miami called his son in New York and said, "I hate to ruin your day, but I have to tell you that your mother and I are divorcing. Forty-five years of misery is enough."

"Pop, what are you talking about?" the son asked in disbelief.

"We can't stand the sight of each other any longer," the old man said. "We're sick of each other, and I'm sick of talking about this. So you call your sister in Chicago and tell her." Then he hung up.

Frantic, the son called his sister, who exploded. "There's no way they're getting divorced!" she shouted. "I'll take care of this." She called Miami immediately and screamed at her father, "You are *not* getting divorced. Don't do a single thing until I get there. I'm calling my brother back, and we'll both be there tomorrow. Until then, don't do a thing. *Do you hear me?*" Then she hung up.

> Members of a family that is based on covenant and lives in an atmosphere of grace and empowering will be able to so communicate and express themselves that they intimately know and are known by one another.
>
> JACK AND JUDITH BALSWICK

The old man hung up his phone too. Turning to his wife with a smile, he said, "OK, honey, they're coming for Thanksgiving. Now what do we do to get them to come home for Christmas?"

It's probably quite clear that this story is fictitious. Although the deception and manipulation in this tale are humorous, they are painful realities for some families. How far back on your family tree do you have to go before you discover family members who brought pain on themselves and others through their choices or behavior? One person—or couple's—actions can wreak havoc for generations of other family members, making it challenging for anyone in the family to find enough to go around.

But one person's—or couple's—actions can also bring great *blessing* to generations of family members. How do our families of origin, our marriage and our parenting help or hinder us in our quest to find more to go around?

Family of Origin

Every family is a miniature civilization with its own unique culture. As youngsters, we tend to assume that our family experience is the norm. But as we mature, we begin to observe vast differences among the personalities and characteristics of families. Although no one grows up in a perfect family, some families are definitely healthier than others. In Dolores Curran's book *Traits of a Healthy Family* she observes that qualities like love, acceptance, shared faith, security, safety, honesty, respect and humor are found in families that desire to serve one another.[1] If these are traits that you saw in your original family, it's likely that you're encouraging them in your current family.

Apparently Scott Spence saw some of these traits in his dad. During the 1999 PGA Gold Tournament, several golf pros were interviewed about what they carried in their golf bags. The most unusual response came from Spence, who divulged that he carried a jar containing some of his father's cremated remains. "It's nice," said Spence, "to still have him around at a major tournament like this."[2]

Sharon is another person who is grateful for her heritage. The atmosphere in her home was filled with humor and hospitality. Growing up in a high-energy family that had a bundle of fun, Sharon felt that her home was a safe place because each family member was treated with respect. The family talked about anything and everything—sometimes simultaneously, without considering it rude. Her family had their problems, but they were dealt with in a reasonable and straightforward manner. Sharon knew that her parents had some disagreements, but she also saw that disagreements and hurts could be worked through maturely.

Janet, however, doesn't have many fond childhood memories. Her family was very private—with good reason. Although her mother was a kind, hardworking woman, her father was an alcoholic. When sober, Janet's father was pleasant to have around, but when he had been drinking, life was frightening—like the night he pushed his wife down the stairway. As a result Janet and her siblings spent lots of time away from home. They avoided having friends over to their house. It was just too risky.

In addition to the unhealthy, unspoken rules "don't speak, don't trust, don't feel," there were several family secrets.

We tend to automatically re-create our family of origin when we marry and establish a family of our own; this is how cross-generation patterns are formed. The more we know about our family, the more we know about ourselves. With that knowledge, we can be more intentional about the family we are establishing. Unfortunately, women who live with unresolved issues from their original family carry resentment and feel that there's not enough to go around in their present family. They often experience the ongoing emotional drain that results from tension and severed relationships.

Taking time to understand our past is one step toward building a healthier future. You may remember with gratitude the nurture and love you received from your family of origin. Or, like Janet, you may regret that problems from your family of origin are continuing to cause challenges for you even now. How do we approach unresolved issues from our family of origin so that we can find more to go around in our present family?

> *It is assumed that the capacity of an individual to function as a spouse and a parent is largely a consequence of childhood relationships in the family of origin.*
> FROMA WALSH

Prayer —Hope Amidst Heartache

Even the very *first* family in the world had serious family problems. Early in Genesis 4 we read that Cain hated his brother Abel so much that he killed him. It should come as no surprise to us, then, that the first reference to prayer in the Bible is found at the end of this same chapter. "At that time men began to call on the name of the LORD" (Genesis 4:26). There's nothing like the heartache of family problems to bring us to our knees in prayer.

After the dismal news of Cain's murder, Eve and Adam may have felt as if all hope was gone, but that was not the case. Hope was on the way. God gave Adam and Eve a third son, Seth, who, according to Luke 3:38, was an ancestor of Jesus Christ. And when God sent Jesus down to earth to be Immanuel (God with us), where did he place him? In a family.

Although the tapestry of family life in the Bible includes flawed people with every imaginable problem, it also includes great hope for blessing. For us today, the news is even more hopeful. Our families of origin also include flawed people with every imaginable problem. But because of our faith in the death and resurrection of Jesus (who came through the line of Seth), not only do we find help for those problems when we call on God, but he gives us the presence of his Spirit to walk through the problems with us.

Perfectionism — Give It Up!

Realizing that there is no such thing as a perfect family and that we will not experience perfection this side of heaven, we seek to cultivate family relationships that reflect God's love and grace.

One mom said, "I realize that every human relationship will disappoint; we all at times fail each other. Only God's relationship to us will not. As a result, I see grace as the God-given means to make up the difference of what each relationship lacks. He can fill us with his forgiveness and love."[3] God's guidance helps reenergize our relationships at times when we feel like there isn't enough to go around.

Surprisingly, sometimes it is people who grew up in the least healthy families who form the most idealistic expectations of family life. Because their childhood was chaotic, they may attempt to create perfection in their present family. These people tend to be unforgiving of their own imperfections.

Betsy grew up in an alcoholic family and struggled with anxiety related to her sense of personal inadequacy. These anxieties were compounded when her young family relocated several times due to her husband's corporate assignments. Though she was an extremely capable woman with a graduate degree in education and functioned as a loving and attentive mother, she couldn't live up to her own expectations.

> *Accept life with humility and patience, making allowances for each other because you love each other.*
> EPHESIANS 4:2
> (PHILLIPS)

She overlooked her strengths and capabilities and became depressed about her slightest imperfections.

When she became aware of these tendencies and distorted beliefs, she worked hard to overcome them. Betsy began to grow in confidence, even during her husband's frequent business trips. As Betsy became more confident, she was less anxious and needed less reassurance. She began to flourish in her varied roles, and her children benefited from her example. Confident and well-adjusted, she and her children now embark on their lives from a more secure foundation, and they're all finding more resilience to meet life's demands.

Getting out of the Rut

If you grew up in a reasonably healthy family, if your present family is functioning well and if you consider yourself to be well adjusted, there's no necessity to look under a microscope for pathology or to seek counseling. But if your family of origin lived with unhealthy patterns that continue to haunt you, or you're experiencing difficulties in your present relationships, consider seeking professional help. You may be encouraged to hear that the healthier a family member is, the quicker he or she is to break out of silence and secrets to seek the outside help of a pastor, counselor or wise friend.

In order to make a wise and careful choice, ask a trusted pastor or friend to direct you to someone who integrates biblical truth with recognized psychological training and expertise. Beware of pop psychology promoting human thought that is outside the scope of God's truth. On a first visit to a counselor, inquire about professional training and qualifications as well as basic beliefs, assumptions and methods. It's important to trust a counselor and feel comfortable with him or her. I (Joan) remind my clients that they need to sense the right chemistry if the process is to be beneficial.

Not long ago it was the trend to look for dysfunction in families, viewing each member as the adult child of some sort of dysfunction. This implied that if we were alive and breathing we either were the product of an unhealthy family or were currently functioning in an unhealthy role. When carried to an extreme, this suggested that we didn't need to take responsibility for our life because we were victims of someone else's mistakes or ignorance.

We need to avoid accepting a victim identity—victims are defeated by their circumstances. Survivors grow through adversity and, with God's help, become conquerors. "In all these things we are more than conquerors through him who loved us" (Romans 8:37). Even though Grandpa may have gambled away the family fortune, his children and grandchildren can make much better choices.

Exiting the Eggshells

In its balanced state, a family is like a mobile suspended in space—a thing of beauty. But if one component is unbalanced, the whole mobile hangs askew. In similar fashion, an unhealthy member of a family can exert tremendous influence and control over the entire family system. Frequently the rest of the family adapts to the behavior of the unhealthy individual. A classic example is the alcoholic family where the substance abuser is enabled to continue his or her drinking as long as the supporting cast continue to play their roles. Even though it may not be possible to change the behavior of an unhealthy family member, his or her impact is greatly diminished when other family members begin to look honestly at the painful situation and take responsibility for their lives.

Thirty-year-old Sheri spent a difficult week with her parents. As usual, Sheri's father treated her mother harshly and disrespectfully. Many times in the past Sheri's dad had ruined family outings, but this time she wasn't going to ignore his hurtful behavior. At the close of the week, Sheri told her father how hurt she was that he had been cruel to her mother.

It wasn't easy for Sheri to confront her dad. She was so nervous that she trembled when she spoke to him. Afterward, though, she respected herself for speaking the truth in love. As she continued to do it when necessary, she noticed that her father's respect for her increased. By caring enough to confront, she was able to effect some change in the unhealthy status quo.

If family members are "walking on eggshells," it's often an indication of the impact one person is having on the whole family. One unhealthy member has the potential to make life miserable for everyone. As long as an unhealthy member controls the family, each individual feels drained and convinced that there isn't enough to go around. But even if your family lived that way in the past, you, like Sheri, can choose to make constructive changes in the present.

Families of origin can be foundations for the development of healthy, well-adjusted individuals, and they can also be sources of intense hurt and pain. As we call on God, stop looking for perfection, get help when necessary and decide not to hand power to unhealthy family members, we begin to discover more wholeness to go around for our present family. With God's presence and help, any family and any parent, at any time, can be the beginning of a healthy Christian heritage.

Marriage

> An archeologist is the best husband any woman can have. The older she gets, the more he is interested in her!
> AGATHA CHRISTIE

If every family is a miniature civilization, then every marriage is a crosscultural experience. We each bring the background and expectations of our family of origin. We are a blend of our parents' backgrounds, and our children are a blend of ours. In the same way that our parents' marriage affected us, our marriage will affect our children. Whether or not you would have chosen to grow up in your family of origin, the marriage and family you create gives you a chance to reevaluate the past and build constructively for the future.

Marriage was God's idea. He intended it to be a unique and exclusive companionship, asking us to leave our family of origin, pledge our love and commitment to our husband in a lifelong covenant, and experience the most intimate of all human relationships. Because marriage was introduced in the context of a spiritual conflict (Genesis 2—3), we shouldn't be surprised that it includes hard work. Although the work of marriage can never yield perfection, it can result in a healthier relationship that equips and energizes us for other areas of our life. How can we invest in our marriage so that it will promote more to go around?

Communicating with love and respect. In marriage and family counseling, I (Joan) encourage married couples to intentionally set a regular time and place to meet and discuss their "state of the union." It might be Friday afternoons at Starbucks, Saturday mornings on a walk or Sunday evenings over pie and ice cream. The positive results of these times together continue to astound my clients, and many couples have made it an ongoing practice in their marriage. I suggest that these times together begin with affirmation and appreciation and progress to questions such as "Am I meeting your needs?" and "Is there any disagreement or misunderstanding we need to discuss?"

Using "I statements" to voice needs and requests is a good way to help our partner succeed in meeting those needs. This is much healthier than expecting our partner to be a mind reader. Ingrid Trobisch says, "When a woman tells me that if her husband really loved her, he would know why she was hurt, I have to go to his defense and say, 'My dear, he doesn't have a clue unless you tell him. Remember, only a baby has the right to be understood without words, not a grown woman.'"[4] If we've asked our husband for something and he meets our request, we need to be careful not to devalue his work by saying, "Too bad I had to ask for it." This puts him in a no-win situation.

Beth and Ray are great examples of setting each other up for success. Beth praised the way Ray remembered special occasions with appropriate cards, flowers or gifts. Ray didn't allow himself to receive all the credit. With a smile, he said, "What Beth's not telling you is that at the beginning of each year, she entered all the significant dates in my Day-timer!"

Our friends Bruce and Ruthie make it their goal—every day—to do at least one thing that will help make the other's life easier. Their marriage is a beautiful picture of mutual respect. Another friend, Colleen, prays each morning that she will bring her husband, Fred, good—not harm—all the days of his life (Proverbs 31:12). This has helped Colleen to become more encouraging to her husband, and it's also helped her become aware of some things she said and did that were *discouraging*. Praying that she will bring him good doesn't mean that she never disagrees with him. When Fred acts selfishly, part of the good that Colleen does is to speak the truth in love.

> *If love were only a feeling, there would be no basis for the promise to love each other forever.*
> ERICH FROMM

Conflict: Deal with it! Conflict is inevitable in any honest relationship, but nothing makes an atmosphere more tense than unresolved differences. The most common areas of disagreement in marriage pertain to—you guessed it—money, sex and in-laws, although there are many variations on these themes, and these are not the *only* areas of conflict. A couple may develop (or bring from families of origin) the tendency to run away from disagreements. Sometimes conflict is ignored in hopes that it will go away—but it doesn't.

In *Hiding from Love* John Townsend says feelings that are buried are always buried alive.[5] Where there is private pain resulting from a spouse's destructive or addictive behaviors, finding the courage to confront may be extremely difficult, but it is necessary to the growth of both husband and wife. "When prolonged personal sin is discovered in the life of another . . . then we must deal with it. . . . The lingering agony of unresolved concern, the energy sapped in bottling up feelings or denying needs, and the clever games that must be played in order to avoid the confrontation, are rarely worth the short-term pain of dealing with the problem."[6]

Not all wives face such large obstacles, but many still find it difficult to state what's bothering them. Some marriage partners resort instead to the silent treatment or a "snit"—an unhealthy controlling method that drains each partner and compounds the "not enough to go around" syndrome. At times it's even accompanied with a smug satisfaction that nothing mean or harmful has been said. But who says that sins of omission are

Great peace have they who love thy law and nothing shall offend them.
PSALM 119:165 (KJV)

less damaging than sins of commission? Stating our concerns in a loving, straightforward way takes courage and careful thought but elevates our communication to a new level of respect and intimacy.

There are many constructive ways to deal with conflict, but a few simple principles are essential.

1. Choose an appropriate time and place to discuss differences—not in bed at night, not when exhausted and not in the presence of others. Agreeing to postpone a discussion is not the same as walking away from it. Do make sure you carry through with it, though.

2. Respect each other—do not attack one another. Concentrate on issues and behaviors rather than personal characteristics.

3. Be willing to own responsibility for the problem when appropriate, and apologize without ifs, ands or buts.

4. Stay in the present, the here and now. Resist bringing up junk from the past.

5. Try to take the position of the other (even temporarily) and see things from his point of view. Unless you're dealing with an issue of moral integrity, be willing to negotiate and compromise in order to find solutions. Experiment with a temporary solution for a while, and agree to reevaluate later.

6. If you come to a roadblock, seek additional assistance from a pastor, counselor or trusted friend.

7. Avoid all-or-nothing, black-and-white thinking. Stay away from terminal words such as always and never. Look for options and alternatives.

Total agreement on everything isn't necessary in a healthy relationship. It's appropriate to agree to disagree on some issues—especially when these issues have no direct impact on the marriage. When my (Joan's) youngest daughter, Jill, was in grade school, she invited her dear friend Margaret to accompany our family on a vacation to Yellowstone and the Tetons. Idealistic Jill wanted everything to be perfect and was feeling responsible even for the weather. When Jill and Margaret had their first little spat, Jill was devastated. She felt as though the trip had been ruined. Margaret placed her hands on her hips and emphatically proclaimed, "Jill, just because we don't agree doesn't mean we don't like each other!" Margaret's wise words have been quoted by our family ever since.

> *When the ways of people please the LORD, he causes even their enemies to be at peace with them.*
> PROVERBS 16:7
> (NRSV)

"Authentic relationships usually tell a story with ups and downs, good and bad episodes. It is impossible for people to live together without occasionally hurting each other. Forgiveness is the balm that mends the tears in our commitments to each other. Forgiveness is the key difference between stories of bitterness and stories of love."[7]

Are you aware that the ability to work through differences respectfully and effectively is strongly correlated with marital fidelity? Keep short accounts with God and with each other. Learn to bless each other; it's the secret to preventing power struggles that cause endless tension in marriages. Power struggle and emotional intimacy are mutually exclusive—they just don't go together.

Responsibility: Take it. One of the most unrealistic expectations of marriage is that we're able to make our spouse happy or that he is able to do that for us. There would never be enough of us to go around. Taking responsibility for our own happiness contributes to our emotional health. "No two people can hope to gratify all of each other's needs. No man or woman can be all things to another."[8]

A Christian philosophy of marriage accepts the fact that no

marriage will meet all of our emotional needs. If it did, we would not need a relationship with God to satisfy the deepest needs and longings of our hearts. This philosophy is not a "cop-out" to keep us from investing our best energies into marriage in order to make it as strong as it can be. Rather, it is a perspective that helps us accept the inevitable limitations and imperfections of any marriage. It's never fair to expect any one person to make us happy.

Even if you presently feel that you may have married the wrong person, by God's grace you may be able to perceive him as the right person down the road. We know many women who have chosen to remain in difficult (not life-threatening) marriages and who later were incredibly grateful, for a host of reasons, that their marriage had remained intact. The important goal for them was to remain healthy in the midst of an unhealthy situation. This is sometimes a matter of learning to *individuate*—one of my (Joan's) favorite words. To individuate is to separate oneself emotionally and take responsibility for our own happiness and well-being.

A healthy marriage is a balance of dependence and autonomy, a healthy interdependence that allows each individual to be all they are meant to be. An overly dependent woman may initially grant her husband a gratifying sense of feeling needed, but over time he begins to feel that there isn't enough of him to go around. He feels suffocated and wishes that his wife would "grow up." On the other hand, an overly independent wife gives her husband the feeling that he's not necessary or important.

A couple we read about had the right idea. Away for a few days at a teachers' convention, Kelly suddenly remembered that it was Monday, trash day, and she hadn't reminded her husband to take the trashcans out. When Kelly expressed concern to a friend, her friend reminded her that since her husband was at home, he could certainly put out the trash by himself. "But you don't understand," said Kelly. "It takes both of us to take out the trash. I can't carry it and he can't remember it."

Husbands and wives need mutual friends—other couples with similar interests—and they also need separate friends and interests that help balance their "dance of intimacy." For me (Joan) a week of fishing in Canada with my husband would be a week too long, even if I took along a spellbinding book. Likewise, a day of shopping on Michigan Avenue in Chicago would not be Jim's idea of a good time. A secure couple is not threatened if the husband goes on an annual weekend backpacking trip with his buddies, or if his wife takes a trip to an art museum or a play with girlfriends or daughters. Such personal pursuits can ultimately help both wife and husband to be more interesting to each other.

> *Mutual love among the happiest couples does not mean that one derives his or her identity from the other, or that if she starts glockenspiel lessons he does the same, or that they always travel together or have friends only in common.*
> GAIL SHEEHY

Reflecting on the level of importance we're giving to our marriage is essential to our growth, both as persons and as partners. If we've been ignoring our marriage while scattering our energies everywhere else, we'd be wise to cut back on less important things for a season. A healthy, loving marriage is God-honoring, and the benefits reach out to a wide circle of recipients. In the process of growing together we discover that there is more of us to go around—both for ourselves and for others.

Parenting

In the hustle and bustle of our culture, it's not uncommon to hear parents say, "I just don't know what to do with this child!"

Although experiencing that feeling every now and then is to be expected, living with the feeling day in and day out can cause us to become weak, immobilized or even paralyzed.

New parents quickly learn that raising children is kind of desperate improvisation.
BILL COSBY

It's important for us to remember that God is the only perfect parent, and even he has some troubled children. It's also important to remember that "God did not give us a spirit of timidity, but a spirit of power, of love and of self-discipline" (2 Timothy 1:7). Even at times when our fears threaten to immobilize us, God has promised to strengthen us as we trust in him.

Although perfect mothers do not exist, we can seek to be what D. W. Winnicott calls "the goodenough mother."[9] This is a comforting concept for those of us who unrealistically strive for perfection. Amid the busyness of our lives, how can we be "goodenough" moms? When there's not enough to go around, what are the aspects of parenting that we just can't afford to ignore?

Modeling—a parent's career. Christian parents have the privilege of modeling and teaching faith in Christ through daily experiences. But in order for children to follow our teaching, they need to respect us first. "If Christian parents are perceived by a child as not being worthy of respect, then neither is their religion, their morals, or their government, or their country, or any of their values. This becomes the generation gap at its most basic level."[10] Failing to establish this type of respect may result in something like the comment of one well-meaning mother: "The book of Proverbs said my children should rise up and call me blessed, but mine have called me stupid."

Gordon Allport, author of *The Individual and His Religion*, studied faith development in families and reports what many of us have seen to be true in our families and other families as well: what parents modeled regarding their beliefs was much more powerful than what they said. The sincerity of their lives was a large determinant of an enduring faith in their children.[11]

Christian parents have the opportunity of reflecting the nature of God to our children—praying for them, forgiving them and taking responsibility for their spiritual development. As we follow Christ ourselves, we begin to foster a sense of God's presence in our home that promotes natural and comfortable conversation about his goodness in our lives. My (Joan's) heart was warmed late one night when my young son Winsor called me into his bedroom and asked, "How do I know if it's God talking or me thinking?" Winsor is now a pastor, and we are still discussing that question years later!

> *As parents show love, instruction, prayer and words of wisdom, they are making investments and building equity for their children. When the children go off to college and are away from Mom and Dad, they draw from a repository of investments that their parents made during the years at home.*
> **JAY KESLER**

Cherishing—a parent's privilege. We are privileged to meet one of the most basic needs of our children: the need to feel loved and cherished. Cherishing our children means treating them with attention and tenderness; children need both our time and our heart. Perhaps nothing else is as vital to the development of a secure and confident personality. John Bowlby describes this type of parenting as the "secure base from which a child or adolescent can make sorties into the outside world and to which he can return knowing for sure that he will be welcomed when he gets there, nourished physically and emotionally, comforted if distressed, reassured if frightened."[12]

How sad to see the results when parents substitute things and stuff for time with their children. I (Joan) hear the angry adolescents in family therapy. When their parents ask where they have gone awry, when they thought they had given their kids everything, the child's reply is often "Yes, everything but yourself." Perhaps this contributes to the sense of entitlement many young people appear to have today. They seem to feel they are entitled to anything and everything they desire because they've been deprived of what they really needed—more time and love from mom and dad.

Taking charge—a parent's responsibility. Even though we parents sometimes wish we could love our children into responsible maturity, we soon realize that loving our children is not enough. Just as God, who loves us unconditionally, gives us limits for our protection, we also need to set limits for our children. Unfortunately, some parents don't worry about setting limits until their children are completely out of control—or more correctly stated, completely *in* control of the household and the adults. What is more pathetic than seeing a toddler dominate parents who are too insecure to set limits? Parents soon find their world shrinking as family and friends hesitate to invite them over, or pretend that no one is home when the doorbell rings. When parents are too afraid of their children to set and enforce appropriate limits, the parents become helpless and the children become insecure.

Children who are both loved and consistently taught to obey will likely grow up to be secure children. A toddler who knows she is loved and who also learns obedience and respect is on the way to becoming a responsible school-aged child and adolescent. When young children are taught to obey and to respect authority, the teen years do not need to be faced with fear and dread by parents or kids—they can actually be enjoyed.

Diana Baumrind studied parent-child interactions in 110 families over a period of twenty-five years.[13] Her observations about parental nurture, control, communication and expectations helped her identify and evaluate the following three parenting styles.

1. The *permissive* style is high in nurturing, high in communication and low in control. These parents who want to be popular with their kids often give in to peer pressure themselves. Children growing up in these homes tend to lack internalized limits and are prone to impulsive behavior.

2. The *authoritarian* style is high in control, low in nurture and low in communication. It operates on the "because I said so" principle and often fosters rebellion. Unfortunately, Christian couples are sometimes inclined to implement this parenting style. If parents attempt to manipulate their children by using Scripture and prayer to create guilt and compliance, rebellion may not be far behind.

3. The *authoritative style* is high in control, high in nurture and high in communication. This is optimal parenting, where there are limits in the context of love and communication. The positive outcome of this style has been repeatedly documented, with high rates of responsibility and low rates of substance abuse and teen pregnancy.

Which parenting style did you experience while you were growing up? Which style do you find yourself using now? Which style will promote more to go around—for you and your children?

Essentials versus nonessentials. In the midst of school, baseball, ballet, music lessons, church activities and family celebrations, we often let ourselves be controlled by whatever's urgent, forgetting to ask ourselves what's most important. What would happen if we began asking, *For this hour [day, month, year], what's most important?*

As a parent, what things do I want to invest time and money in? Books? Music? Sports? We can't do it all.

What can I simplify? Do I really want to spend thirty hours planning a complicated birthday party for my child if I'm going to be crabby for the next two weeks? Perhaps we'd all be happier if I planned a trip to the local petting zoo or a few innings of baseball at the neighborhood park with cake and ice cream afterward.

Is this a hill to die on? It's easy to make a big deal out of things that aren't going to matter in the long run. On one occasion when I (Joan) was pressing my high school daughter Jill to clean her room, I was startled when she responded, "Mom, please get your priorities straight. I love God. I'm a virgin. I don't do drugs or alcohol, and I have wonderful friends."

At that moment I remembered wise words of my friend Joseph Bayly: "Don't sweat the nonessentials!" For that day, a clean bedroom just wasn't the most important thing. Throughout each day, we need to be asking, "What's most important?"

Seizing teachable moments—a parent's opportunity. Living together provides countless "teachable moments" if we are aware of them and choose to seize the opportunities. Sarah, a young mom whom I (Joan) mentor, was tired of her children's squabbling over who got to sit in the front seat of the car. Deciding that praying was better than squabbling, Sarah seized one teachable moment. She asked her children to write their prayer requests on Post-it notes and stick them on the car's dashboard. Sarah worked out a rotation system and appointed the front-seat passenger as "chaplain" for each day.

The outcome was amazing. One day the kids prayed that they would find four floor mats that had blown off the car roof after they used the car wash and drove away absent-mindedly. Their prayers were answered when they later found the car mats in a snowbank by the side of the road! Seeing an answer to that prayer gave them courage to pray that relatives and neighbors would become Christ-followers, and some of those prayers have been answered too.

I (Ellen) fondly remember one teachable moment with my son Chad about twenty years ago. One lovely summer morning Chad (age four) and I had just returned from the grocery store and unloaded the bags from the car.

Sitting on the back porch steps while Chad finished a snack, we launched into one of those unhurried talks that a mom never forgets. He wondered whom he was going to marry. I explained that was something I did not know, that it depended on women he met and choices he made, and that God could help him in that big decision.

I asked what kind of woman he thought he might *like* to marry. His response was amazing. "She has to love God and bake bread, and she has to be able to keep a secret!" After I affirmed him for his great thoughts, he confidently announced, "When I find her, I'm going to name her Bambi!"[14] I'll enjoy sharing that teachable moment with generations yet to come.

Discovering helpful resources—a parent's lifeline. When she first became a single mom, Bonnie wondered how she would ever find enough to go around. Returning to school to upgrade her LPN to an RN degree meant combining early morning and evening classes with her full-time job. Although Bonnie felt uneasy about spending more time away from her three school-aged children, she believed her study program would help them in the long term, allowing her to provide for them and keep the family together. Having grown up in a series of foster homes and orphanages, Bonnie had no firsthand experience of a healthy home, but she was determined to prevent her early experiences from becoming a cross-generation pattern.

She has succeeded in creating a remarkable degree of family

solidarity as her children have learned how to work hard and share responsibility. Seeking to avoid the "all work and no play" policy, though, she adopted a dog to add energy to the household. She creatively plans educational vacations on a shoestring.

There are no guarantees in marriage or in parenting because our spouses and our children are separate individuals who make choices of their own. That reality ought to call us to even more "knee bends," which are, after all, the very best exercise for true marital and parenting fitness. For when you stop to think about it, God asks us to do with our spouses and children the very thing He asks us to do with our entire lives: release them to Him and rely on His faithfulness.
SANDRA D. WILSON

Bonnie has learned to use available resources without becoming excessively dependent on them. Her children have benefited from community-sponsored day camps, after-school programs, church youth groups and pastors, vocational high school programs and teen mission trips. When her children are grown, she anticipates being able to travel a bit with friends and do some of the things she has put on hold. In the meantime she lives sacrificially for the good of her children. We applaud her and hope that Rose, Nathan and Andrew will rise up and call her blessed (Proverbs 31:28).

The biggest resource available to us as parents, of course, is prayer. Praying with and for our children is a privilege we can combine with our many other tasks at any place and any time. What a comfort to be able to commit them to the care of a loving Father who is always present in their lives.

With God's help, we want to be the best parents we can possibly be. Knowing that we can commit our children to God's care, we pray faithfully for them to love and serve him above all else. As we relinquish the outcome to him, we learn what it really means to trust God.

Reflection Questions

1. Read Genesis 24:1-66. What positive patterns for the family are being modeled and passed down here?

2. Read Genesis 27:1-45. What negative patterns for the family are being modeled and passed down here?

3. What is one positive characteristic from your family of origin that you want to encourage in your present family? What is one characteristic from your family of origin that you would like to change in your present family?

4. How is your marriage similar to and different from your parents'?

5. What does the Bible teach about conflict resolution? Read Galatians 6:1; Ephesians 4:15, 32; 1 Timothy 1:5; 1 Peter 3:8-12; James 1:19.

6. Read Deuteronomy 4:9-10; 6:6-7; Joshua 4:6. What do you learn about modeling and seizing teachable moments?

7. What parenting style did you grow up under? What parenting style are you using now?

8. What has been your most valuable resource for parenting?

7

Fitting Friendships into a Busy Life

Women always need other women to come
alongside and speak their language:
the language of the heart and feelings.

BRENDA HUNTER, *IN THE COMPANY OF WOMEN*

*T*hink of a time in your life when there wasn't enough to go around and you knew that you needed a friend. Maybe you were depressed. Or you had recently moved. Or you were under incredible pressure at work. Or someone in your family was seriously ill. Whatever the circumstances, you knew that you needed the help, perspective and support of a good friend. Yet you may have questioned whether your crowded life could even include time for friendships.

Marlene distinctly remembers two such times. Looking back, she realizes that she learned some lessons about friendship from the first experience that helped her to handle the second one better.

While pregnant with her second child, Marlene was shocked one night to hear her husband say that he was emotionally involved with another woman. Devastated and numb, Marlene retreated inside herself. Although she knew that her husband was being incredibly selfish, she also assumed that there was something terribly wrong with her. She didn't share her problem, or the pain that accompanied it, with her friends, for she feared they would think less of her if they knew how weak and inadequate she felt. During the next months Marlene's husband appeared to see the folly of his ways, but not before Marlene spiraled into a period of depression.

> *A friend is someone to whom I do not have to explain myself. Such a friendship offers unspeakable comfort. Friendships can also be redemptive, for friends can act as mediators of God's presence and invite us into the embrace of God's grace.*
> INGRID TROBISCH

Although she thought that her marriage was on the mend, several years later Marlene received yet more unwelcome news from her husband. Since trying to go it alone hadn't worked in the past, she decided to ask for the help and support of a few close friends this time. Being open and honest, Marlene began to discover a wealth in her friendships that she had never experienced before. With appropriate transparency, her friendships grew deeper and stronger, and she discovered that even though some people might appear to have it all together on the outside, nobody this side of heaven does.

It's important to have friends in every stage of life, but we often feel the need most keenly when we're going through tough times—which we all do.

Years ago Barbra Streisand made popular a song that said, "People who need people are the luckiest people in the world." Actually people who need people are the *only* kind of people in the world, because God made us all for companionship. Women who have friends are healthier, happier, and less depressed and anxious, and they generally have a longer life span. Quality friendships also help us become better wives and mothers. "Connectedness," says Archibald Hart, "is essential to a healthy self."[1] Friendships are clearly an important resource for gaining help and support when there's not enough of us to go around.

Many women have special gifts for developing meaningful friendships—a capacity that often becomes evident in early childhood. Little girls learn early in life to share secrets, have best friends and develop loyalties. Do you remember some of the friends with whom you pretended, played dolls or traded secrets? And who of us can ever forget the first pangs of hurt, rejection or jealousy we experienced in grade school? Nothing was as wonderful as being included and nothing as painful as being left out. The feeling of being left out doesn't necessarily stop in childhood, though. Even queens have been known to feel that way. After the great British poet Alfred, Lord Tennyson visited Queen Victoria in her palace, he commented, "Up there, in all her glory and splendor, she was lonely." The Queen had fame, fortune and fine china, but she seems not to have had enough friends.

In spite of all the commercials suggesting that communication technologies keep family and friends connected, loneliness is epidemic in our society. It is a huge obstacle for women who are trying to find more to go around. Cell phones and e-mail do not alleviate the heart-wrenching feelings of isolation that many women experience. You may feel this way yourself.

Loneliness is just one facet of the depression that often brings women to Joan's counseling office. Some women can't seem to get connected or get along with friends they already have. Others seek help in finding new friends.

At this point, you may be thinking, *I agree that I need to be growing healthy friendships, but how will they promote more of me*

to go around, and how do I pursue them when I'm already busy?
Let's take a look at how other women have found more to go
around both in and through their friendships.

Doing Lunch — The Pause That Refreshes

When I (Ellen) was a young mom in my early thirties, I found
it a challenge just to add one extra thing to any day. In addition
to the daily jobs of caring for my husband and small sons,
cooking, doing laundry and keeping the house running
smoothly (not so smoothly some days), there were other things
to be done, like grocery shopping, church activities and preschool. Amid all the busyness, I tried to plan connections with
a friend once or twice a week. Often it involved going to the
park with all of our children. It was definitely worth the effort.
While the children played, we moms caught up on the latest
happenings in our lives. Visiting with another mom helped me
to know that I wasn't the only mom who was frustrated with
temper tantrums or potty training. I came away from those
moments of connection with my friends feeling more normal.

Now in my early fifties, I continue to have lunch with my
friends. The cuisines are a bit fancier and we go to lunch without the kids, but the common denominator is that we still
come away feeling more normal. We realize that we're not the
only one who dreads the loud music and mess that college students produce upon returning home for the summer. Other
times we cry about the kids who are just leaving for college.
Sometimes we sigh together about signs and symptoms of
menopause. Whatever the topics of any particular day, being
reassured and validated about our feelings and experiences
helps us return to our individual lives with fresh perspective
and renewed energy.

Renewed Friendships Recharge Us

Renewed friendships from childhood sometimes recharge us when our batteries feel like they're running low. I (Joan) experience this when reuniting with friends I made during my schooldays in China. Having attended ten schools before graduating from high school, I can still get stomach pangs from recalling the experience of being the "new girl" time after time. I wondered whether other girls would speak to me, invite me to sit at their table in the lunchroom or include me in recess jump rope. In retrospect, my experiences then probably contributed to my ease in meeting and enjoying people of all types now, but at the time it certainly was not fun!

> *It isn't about the food, really, or where you go, what you wear or who you see there, though those are all parts of it. It's about everything surrounding the meal as happening, event, a way of touching souls. It's about what it really means to be a friend. For me, having lunch with my women friends is ultimately and intimately about survival.*
> MICHELE WELDON

Though my childhood friends from China are presently scattered around the globe, I feel an inexplicable sense of closeness when I reunite with them. The retelling of stories amid laughter and tears seems to reconnect us even after years of being apart. I recently attended a reunion in China. Stories of stays in World War II concentration camps and harrowing evacuations were interspersed with memories of childhood mischief and merriment. The stories and experiences we shared led to a special form of bonding. Even though years have gone by with not much more contact between us than Christmas cards, the renewal of our friendships sent us all home encouraged and reminded of God's faithfulness and goodness in our lives. Being able to stay in touch with friends from different contexts and phases of our lives is an ever-widening blessing.

Shared Interests Enrich Our Lives

Years ago, women who participated in old-fashioned quilting groups and sewing circles were sewing more than just quilts; they were also sowing the seeds of group therapy long before anyone gave it that label! Women today may share interests such as tennis, cooking, photography, pottery or needlework. Linda is one of my (Ellen's) special-interest friends. Linda and I share a love of music. Our friendship began twenty-four years ago when I invited her over for lunch. Through the years we have given recitals together and spent afternoons playing through sonatas for violin and piano. In the process we discovered that we had more in common than our interest in music.

> A knowledge that another has felt as we have felt, and seen things not much otherwise than we have seen them will continue to the end to be one of life's choicest blessings.
> ROBERT LOUIS STEVENSON

Although Linda's family moved out of state years ago, we recently renewed our friendship during a weekend in Grand Rapids, Michigan, when we attended a piano teachers' convention. When Linda's mom died, I was able to attend her memorial service not only as a friend but also to appreciate the beautiful music Linda played on the piano.

Mentors Show Us the Way

Another type of friendship that helps fortify us at times when there isn't enough to go around is a cross-generation mentoring friendship. Mentors are special encouragers and guides along life's way who have either lived a little longer than we have or had more experience in some aspect of living, loving or working. They come alongside (usually by invitation) and give nurture, wise counsel and encouragement while serving as role models. Mentoring friendships are not intended to replace the relationship of a mother and daughter but rather to complement it.

More and more young women have sought out mentoring relationships in recent years. Could this be happening because young women are blazing new trails in career options as well as balancing families and careers? I (Joan) frequently interact with college women who feel they are embarking on uncharted waters without role models. Through the years I have maintained mentoring relationships with some of my former students and advisees. Several of these women come from a distance for an annual "mother-daughter" weekend in my home. Others who live nearby meet me for a monthly breakfast. As they have become competent and confident women in various roles, they have imparted much to my life. Their developing personhood, as well as their personal faith, is beautiful to observe, and I am enriched by these relationships. Mentoring is definitely a two-way street.

> *Because we are unconnected by blood, our words of advice are accepted as wise, not intrusive, and our childish lapses don't summon up warnings and groans.*
> JUDITH VIORST

It seems wise to begin a mentoring relationship by agreeing to a specified period of time—perhaps six months. This gives both parties an opportunity to get to know one another and then reevaluate. A mentoring relationship may develop into an enduring friendship, but beginning with a specified time frame protects us from feeling so overwhelmed that we wouldn't even try to participate. If every relationship required an indefinite time commitment, there wouldn't be enough of us to go around.

Not all mentoring, though, is done through formal agreements or get-togethers. Some mentoring takes place by observation. I (Joan) experienced this type of mentoring with my friend Ginger's mother, Henrietta VanDerMolen. Whether Henrietta was sewing for a school benefit bazaar, volunteering in a resale shop that benefits a Christian youth center, organizing a group of people to help in an orphanage in the Ukraine or sharing her home with an unwed mother, she led more by example than by words.

During her twenty-five years as a widow, Henrietta opened her home to forty-six unwed mothers and twenty-seven Russian refugees. She managed both her time and money by David Livingstone's life principle:

> I will place no value on anything I have or may possess except in its relation to the Kingdom of God. If anything I have will advance the interest of that Kingdom, it shall be given up or kept; as by giving or keeping it I shall most promote the glory of Him to whom I owe all my hopes both for time and eternity. May grace be given to me to adhere to this.[2]

She was a great role model because her priorities were focused on the eternal. Though most mentoring relationships are intentionally developed by mutual consent, Henrietta was a mentor to me without even knowing it.

Close Friendships Strengthen Us

Across the sweeping landscape of life, differing levels of friendships are made at various ages and stages. We need a wide circle of acquaintances as part of our sense of knowing and being known. But we also need a few close, ongoing friendships that permit the kind of emotional intimacy our hearts long for. Erich Fromm writes in *The Art of Loving* that the "worst kind of loneliness is to feel lonely when you are with someone you'd like to feel close to."[3] The problem he describes involves not physical separation or distance but emotional disconnection— a lack of true intimacy.

How many close friends do you have? If the answer is more than a small number, you might need to reconsider what constitutes a close friendship. There simply isn't enough of us to go around for cultivating and maintaining more than a few intimate friendships in which we trust (feel safe), share our thoughts and feelings, feel affirmed, accept reality checks and reciprocate these benefits.

Two women in the New Testament (who must at times have felt as if there wasn't enough of them to go around) demonstrated this invaluable kind of close friendship. In their common values and interests, in listening and sharing, in time spent together, and in loyalty and encouragement, Mary and Elizabeth left us a powerful example (see Luke 1:39-56).

Common interests and values. Two thousand years before the development of ultrasounds, Mary and Elizabeth knew that deep inside each of their wombs they were carrying honored sons. Mary was carrying the Son of God, Elizabeth was carrying a prophet of God, and each woman had a story to tell about the visit of an angel. Elizabeth and Mary had a lot in common.

As in their experience, women who are seeking close friendships today are most likely to bond with other women who share similar interests, such as faith, walking, music, photography, children or gardening (for starters!). Joining a women's Bible study, participating in a music group, volunteering at a child's school are some ways to seek out new friends. When we interact with women in a group, we may meet some whom we'd like to get to know better. As we reflect on the history of our close friendships, we often realize that most of them begin with group activities and progress to one-on-one activities.

Casual acquaintanceship may easily accommodate different beliefs and values, but the closest of friendships generally do not. Since what we believe about God, ourselves and others influences the life choices we make, it's unlikely that the term "kindred spirit" would describe a close friendship not built on similar beliefs. If faith in God is important to us, we usually seek advice on issues of the heart from friends who know God and value the same things we value.

That was certainly the case for Elizabeth and Mary. They couldn't wait to share the joys of what God was doing in each of their lives. And they also needed the encouragement of another believer at a time when their lives felt like they had been turned upside down.

Listening and sharing. Mary, a young virgin, had seen an angel who told her that she would become pregnant with God's child by the power of God's Spirit. Who could Mary talk to? Who would ever believe her? . . . Elizabeth would! Elizabeth, whose womb was barren until God delivered news to her husband—also through an angel—that she would conceive and bear a son who would be great in the sight of God. Elizabeth would understand, and Mary needed to share her joys and fears with a woman who did. As the two women prepared meals and washed clothes together, there was probably a lot of listening and sharing going on.

> *The human heart, at whatever age, opens only to the heart that opens in return.*
> MARIA EDGEWORTH

In a close friendship we listen all the time, not just with our ears but with our mind, our eyes and our heart—even during silences. Stephen R. Covey, author of the bestselling *The Seven Habits of Highly Effective People,* notes that there are five levels of listening: ignoring, pretend listening, selective listening, attentive listening and empathetic listening. The last level is the only one in which the listener puts herself in the other person's frame of reference.

Close friendships include sharing that is mutual, because we don't risk transparency on a regular basis with a friend who wouldn't think of telling us what's going on in her world. Self-disclosure needs to be reciprocal if we are to grow a balanced friendship. Though we may pride ourselves on being a good listener, if we withhold our thoughts and feelings, our friendships won't have very far to grow.

> *If we find we are too busy for friends, we must conclude we are too busy.*
>
> *Life is a façade if it speeds past the lasting in pursuit of the transient.*
>
> GLORIA GAITHER, PEGGY BENSON AND JOY MACKENZIE

Spending time together. The Bible doesn't say that Mary *went* to visit Elizabeth—it tells us that she *hurried.* What a greeting they must have shared! Mary had traveled one hundred miles, probably on a donkey, to be with Elizabeth, and she stayed with her for about three months. Ninety days is a rather long visit, but these women both needed the gift of each other's time.

Today, finding time for our friends is a big challenge. Although we have much to give and receive in friendship, our crowded, busy lives often prohibit the relationships we need and desire. We need to get creative—and realistic—about ways to connect with our friends. If we can't see them every week, what about scheduling a special lunch once a month? Some women we know volunteer as youth leaders one night a week and go out together for pie and coffee afterward. I (Ellen) like to combine walking and talking with my friends. Some moms choose to teach Sunday school together. I (Joan) meet friends for lunch when I'm attending conferences and professional meetings.

Deep connections grow little by little, not overnight. A woman who approaches friendship with too much intensity can frighten others away. Carrie, a young mom, had a pattern of building intense friendships with women while making draining demands on them. Inevitably the relationships were short-lived once people began to feel used. People around Carrie typically distanced themselves from her in self-defense. It was sad to see her circle of available friends shrink over the years. While we need to devote enough time to growing close friendships, we are wise not to expect too much too soon. It's best to let friendships unfold naturally.

One woman reflects on how her trio of friendship progressed:

> Ours was a friendship molded by years. It began back when the men baby-sat so the women could squeeze in a night of bridge. It spanned school plays, soccer games, dance recitals and graduations. Together we made cinnamon rolls and grew tomatoes and carved out careers. One night Karen had a dinner party, with artichokes as the first course. She taught us to peel away the layers, then dip each petal in the melted butter and scrape off that sweet meat. "You may think you have the best the plant has to offer," she told us. "But the best is yet to come. Because when you've peeled away all of your layers, you'll find the heart of the artichoke, the gift of the plant."
>
> What Karen said about the artichoke can also be said about friendship. We peel away the layers, one at a time, until finally we reach the heart of a person.[4]

Close friendships take time.

Loyalty and encouragement. Luke 1:45 records that Elizabeth said to Mary, "Blessed is she who has believed that what the Lord has said to her will be accomplished!" Mary must have had a high level of trust in Elizabeth to tell her what God said to her. Elizabeth's response was beautiful. She encouraged Mary's faith.

Mary's words must also have encouraged Elizabeth, because at that time Elizabeth couldn't converse with her husband, Zechariah. (God had silenced the lips of Zechariah until the birth of his son, John, as a consequence of Zechariah's unbelief.) What a gracious provision this friendship was for both women. "In the Bible friendship is a mutual improvement activity, honing one for godly use. Biblical friendship is a face-to-face encounter, signifying proximity, intimate revelation and honesty. It is also a bonding of affections and trust, knitting one's very soul to another."[5]

Loyalty in our close friendships involves trust, faithfulness and dependability. Mary never would have confided in Elizabeth or stayed with her for ninety days if she didn't trust her. We trust that our close friends will never betray us, or betray our confidences to other people. How many friendships have been ruined because someone repeated information that never should have been repeated? Proverbs 16:28 reminds us that gossip separates the best of friends.

It is one of the main duties of friends to help one another to be better persons: one must hold up a standard for one's friend and be able to count on a true friend to do likewise.

ROBERT DELLAII

Our close friends are loyal enough that when they are bothered by something in our life they'll come to us and speak the truth in love, as opposed to discussing it with someone else. Giving—or receiving—the gift of honesty is no easy task. But if we avoid the giving and receiving of honest concerns, we miss out on an important ingredient of close friendship. Speaking the truth in love must always be done graciously. If our words deteriorate into "brutal honesty," we'll end up doing more harm than good.

In a church committee meeting, Sue was irritated that her friend Kim had spoken rudely to another committee member. This wasn't the first time she'd heard Kim talk like that. Sue appreciated her friendship with Kim and had wished on similar occasions that she had courage to talk to her about the impact her words had on others.

The next day Sue decided that she would speak to Kim about her feelings. She was nervous but knew it was the right thing to do. First Sue affirmed Kim for her contributions to the committee and thanked her for their friendship. Then she brought up the hurtful comment the night before.

At first, Kim was a little defensive, but after a few minutes she said, "You know, I probably needed to hear that." Not only did the mutual respect level between the two women go up a notch, but a few weeks later Sue received the following note in the mail:

> Dear Sue,
> You are an encouragement to me. A couple of verses come to my mind when I think of you—verses that talk about building each other up and speaking the truth in love. Thanks for not ignoring things in my life that need attention, but also for encouraging me when it's appropriate. You have credibility in my eyes because of our long-standing friendship, but also because I know that God has used challenges in your life to push you closer to him.
> Your sister in Christ,
> Kim

Speaking the truth in love—and receiving the truth in love—can lead to new levels of loyalty in our friendships.

Close friends are also encouraging, like Mary and Elizabeth.

Ingrid Trobisch describes close friends as those who cheer us on when we have high mountains to climb and comforters for when we fall. "They are my sounding board and feedback. They listen carefully when I tell my story and offer quiet nuggets of wisdom that give light for the next step. I know I can count on them always to be there when I need them. . . . These friends accept me just the way I am, but like Christ, they don't leave me that way. They help me to break out of my walls of self-pity and discouragement."[6] How blessed we are if we have friends who are both loyal and encouraging. May we seek to be that kind of friend. "The wonderful truth of the gospel is that we can be equipped for friendship, not primarily by taking a crash course in 'interpersonal skills' or by reading 'self-help' books, but by allowing the Lord Jesus to work in our lives to enable us to become the right persons."[7]

Balancing the Give and Take

As you reflect on your friendships, are you able to identify friends that help you and friends you minister to? You probably have some in each category. It's important to intentionally maintain a balance over time. People who have a need to rescue may seek out needier friends—but over the long haul they are likely to burn out. We also need friends we can hurry to and confide in as Mary did with Elizabeth.

Our capacity to extend care to others and our need to receive nurture are not always constant but tend to ebb and flow with the seasons and circumstances of life. Accepting both of these roles helps us live a balanced life, and finding the proper balance is something we can all work on.

Jesus, the friend of sinners, often allowed his days on earth to be interrupted by the needs of people around him. Just before a large crowd of hungry people followed him to a hill-side, Jesus had received news that John the Baptist had been beheaded. Jesus and his disciples got into a boat and set off to find a solitary place. Most of us would have done the same thing. When we receive bad news, we often want to get away from the hustle and bustle of activity to think, reflect and pray. When Jesus and his disciples arrived at the hillside, though, they were met with a hungry, needy crowd. What was Jesus' response? He "had compassion on them, because they were like sheep without a shepherd" (Matthew 9:36).

All through the biblical accounts Jesus is interrupted by needy people—the sick, the blind, the lame, lepers, prostitutes, cheating tax collectors, people who are confused, hungry and thirsty. He takes time to listen, talk, touch, pray and heal. What an example of compassion and care!

Like Jesus, we ought to involve ourselves in some friend-ships where we don't expect much in return. In his classic little book *Life Together* Dietrich Bonhoeffer writes, "We must not spare our hand where it can perform a service and we must not assume that our schedule is our own to manage, but allow it to be arranged by God."[8] Allowing God to interrupt our day with people and their needs may temporarily compound our sense of "not enough to go around" but will ultimately reward us with a sense of having been an instrument of healing and encouragement.

Annie remembers such a day. A few summers ago she and her daughters took a trip to the South with her husband, who needed to attend a convention. She had been looking forward to relaxing away from the busy demands of her life at home. While sitting by the hotel pool for a couple of hours one after-noon, Annie casually mentioned to her daughters that she needed to figure out where the laundry room was. Another woman sitting by the pool overheard her and kindly gave her the directions she needed. The other woman, Tonya, told Annie that she had been attending the same convention as Annie's husband. Then she mentioned that she was having a difficult day. Exactly one year earlier to the day, her forty-year-old daughter had died of cancer.

Annie sat down next to Tonya, listened to her story, shed tears with her and assured her of her prayers. What Annie hadn't realized was how much God would encourage *her* by using her to encourage Tonya.

We've heard all our life that it's more blessed to give than to receive (Acts 20:35), so we generally assume that giving is the harder of the two. But sometimes it also takes humility and grace to be on the receiving end. Maybe you've been denied the joy of supporting a friend during a difficult period because she couldn't accept help. Or perhaps you've denied your friends opportunities for reaching out to you by giving the appearance that you have it all together all of the time.

Lisa's friends counted on her to be an eternal optimist, looking on the bright side and encouraging others out of the resources of her confident, outgoing personality. Her friends liked to remind her that she lived a charmed life. No wonder her friends were concerned one day when Lisa arrived a bit late for lunch at their favorite restaurant, her eyes red and swollen from crying. They all leaned in close around the table as Lisa shared the results she'd just received from a breast biopsy.

Grieved by the news, her friends surrounded her with love and support, feeling grateful that they could be there in her hour of need as she had so often been for them. Lisa's friends continued to be thankful in the weeks and months following that lunch that they were able to listen, encourage and empathize, and Lisa graciously accepted their help. Without her friends she wouldn't have had enough to go around.

Our friend Dori has seen hundreds of God's provisions delivered through her friends during some very difficult years. A young mom with two delightful children, Dori became a widow after spending three and a half years caring for her husband, Jeff, who had tumors growing in his central nervous system. Although Dori acknowledges how difficult those years were, she is quick to speak of the myriad ways God provided for her family through friends.

☐ He sent people to care for the children. One day Audy walked by the house and asked Dori if she could do anything to help. Dori mentioned that she needed someone to stay with the children before school the next morning while Jeff was in surgery. Audy had *only* that particular spot in her day available.

☐ When Jeff was on steroids and ravenously hungry, God prompted friends and neighbors to drop off meals, pies and groceries each time their cupboards were bare.

☐ Friends helped with laundry and meals. Some people even dropped off secret gifts of flowers, money and toys. Others helped with transportation, driving Jeff to radiation or rehabilitation and taking the kids to soccer practice.

☐ When Kristin's bedroom walls needed some help, friends came to strip wallpaper and paint.

☐ After Jeff's death, God surrounded Dori and the children with quality financial planners, pastoral support and friends to love them.

☐ One winter day Dori took the children skiing, and the three of them returned home exhausted. A heavy snow fell later that night, and none of them wanted to go outside and shovel. The next thing they knew, they heard a motor. Looking out the window, they discovered that their neighbor was snowblowing their driveway!

God has used friends to meet some of Dori's family's most important needs and even a few of their wants. One verse that has meant a lot to Dori is Psalm 34:8: "O taste and see that the LORD is good; happy are those who take refuge in him!" (NRSV).

Friendships Are Worth the Effort

No doubt you face various joys and challenges within your circle of friends. Perhaps while one of your children was in the hospital, you were blessed with friends who showered you with meals, cards and extra love. Or maybe you recently moved, and your heart is aching for a new friend while you're missing the friends you left behind. You may have a friend who's calling you three times a day, and you're sensing the need to establish some limits for the sake of your sanity as well as the health of the friendship. Perhaps you're longing to build a close friendship because you don't have one; you're wondering if close friendships are even possible. Whatever your situation, you're not alone. We all deal with such challenges in our friendships at various times in our lives.

Whether we're listening, sharing, putting a lunch date on the calendar, seeking out a mentor, encouraging a friend or accepting help from another, the work of friendship is definitely worth the effort. As our friendships grow healthier, we are enriched—finding that there's more to go around.

Reflection Questions

1. Was there ever a time when you retreated from life and avoided your friends? If so, what happened?

2. Recount how one of your close friendships began.

3. What is one quality that you value in a close friend?

4. Read Luke 1:26-80. What is one thing you appreciate about the friendship between Mary and Elizabeth? How did God provide for Elizabeth and Mary within the context of their friendship?

5. In what ways has God provided friends for you?

6. Read Luke 10:25-37. How does Jesus ask us to treat needy people around us?

7. How has a friend encouraged you?

8. Read John 15:9-17 and Psalm 25:14. What do we need to do to become friends with God?

9. What is one way you can make time for your friends?

10. Was there ever a time when caring confrontation was helpful to you? Was there ever a time when you were confronted without love and care? If so, how did you feel?

11. How do healthy friendships contribute to our having more to go around?

8

Hope When There Just Isn't Enough to Go Around

Yet this I call to mind
  and therefore I have hope:
Because of the LORD's great love we are not consumed,
  for his compassions never fail.
They are new every morning;
  great is your faithfulness. . . .
The LORD is good to those whose hope is in him.

LAMENTATIONS 3:21-23, 25

*I*t was two weeks before my (Joan's) first grandchild was due. The baby's antique cradle was assembled, the nursery walls had been stenciled, and a sense of happy anticipation prevailed. Jim and I were planning to call our expectant daughter, Jan, on her birthday—but she called us first. We both happened to be home, and answered simultaneously on separate phone extensions.

The news of the next few moments left us stunned with disbelief. After struggling to be reassuring and promising to drive the two hundred miles to Jan's home the next day, we hung up and met in the hallway. "Did we really just hear what I thought we did?" Tears and fears followed.

Jan had just been to the hospital for a routine prenatal ultrasound and had been told that her baby girl would be born with a spinal cord defect, spina bifida. The extent of the infant's paralysis would not be known until her birth, which was scheduled by caesarean two weeks later.

The night before the birth, Jim and I made the trip down to Jan's home once again. Rising at 5:00 a.m. the next morning, we drove Jan and Wayne to the University of Indiana Hospital for the scheduled delivery. All four of us had heavy hearts. As we were reminded of Paul Tournier's words that God does not remove us from the tragedy of life but walks with us through it, we began to experience God's supernatural presence and comfort.

The anesthesiologists came to Jan's room but waited out in the hallway until our family finished praying. Upon entering, one of the doctors empathized with Jan and Wayne, telling them that he had a two-year-old with cerebral palsy. He mentioned that he was reassured by hearing our prayers because he too was a Christ-follower.

When Jan was taken to the operating room, her husband and her obstetrician father were allowed to accompany her. I was left alone in Jan's room to try to find some comfort by reading Psalms. Time seemed endless.

At one point, into the room walked a woman wearing a white lab coat who introduced herself as a resident physician in high-risk obstetrics. She explained that she had met Jan through mutual friends when Jan was a pharmacy student; Jan had subsequently done occasional childcare and housework for her. As she offered me her support, I learned that angels sometimes appear in white lab coats.

When beautiful, blond, blue-eyed Hilary was born paralyzed from her waist down, the words of the pediatric neurosurgeon— which will never be forgotten—were "Grandmother, you have to know that there is much more to a child than her legs!" My eyes still well up with tears as I write these words, because the truth of them has been apparent every day for the past fourteen years. Soon afterward I began a journal entitled "Grandmother's Good Glimpses of God," to record the evidences of God's loving presence as Hilary's life unfolds—because he has truly been a "refuge and strength, an ever-present help in trouble" (Psalm 46:1).

The pain doesn't go away. Hilary is not able to join our active, outdoorsy extended family in tennis, skiing, backpacking or skating. But she has enjoyed whitewater rafting, tobogganing and horseback riding. To my amazement, Hilary once struggled to the top of a large jungle gym, exclaiming, "See, Grammy, I can do anything!" Hilary's love for music enriches her life and the lives of her family as she sings and plays piano and French horn.

Our life is full of brokenness—broken relationships, broken promises, broken expectations. How can we live with that brokenness without becoming bitter and resentful except by returning again and again to God's faithful presence in our lives?
HENRI NOUWEN

Hilary has helped our extended family become better people, as we have learned to slow down and become much more aware of the needs of the disabled. In this experience I have gained a deeper appreciation for what it meant for God to suffer the agony of his Son's death by crucifixion. Is there any greater pain than that of a parent for the suffering of their child or grandchild? I've often said to Jan, "Honey, I'd die on the spot if I could spare you and Hilary this pain."

Jan once replied, "Mother, you are bearing the pain of three generations—yours, mine and Hilary's." It's true.

We live with the hope and assurance that someday Hilary will outrun us all! In the meantime our lives are richer because of her, and we eagerly await what God has in store for her life.

"For I know the plans I have for you," declares the LORD, "plans to prosper you and not to harm you, plans to give you hope and a future." (Jeremiah 29:11)

More Than Enough Heartache to Go Around

We don't need to look far before we see that disappointment and loss are inevitable. Though we all expect to encounter some difficulty in life, we're never sure what it will look like. Sometimes pain presents itself in the form of lingering disappointments, like a debilitating illness. Or we might have a child whose special needs become more apparent as the child grows, bringing new awareness of loss and increased grieving with each passing year. For some it is a public tragedy, like the untimely death of a child or a house fire. In these situations there is often an outpouring of support and comfort from family and friends. Other women experience the hidden sufferings of a difficult marriage or a parent's psychiatric hospitalization. Less support is usually available for dealing with these more private pains. Can we make any sense of all this pain? It's clear that there's plenty of heartache to go around, but how can we find enough hope to go around?

One of the strongest images or metaphors of hope in the Bible is the anchor. In the ancient world, an anchor meant the difference between life and death to those who were at sea. If sailors had a firm anchor, they felt secure even in a storm. Hebrews 6:19 assures us that Christ is the secure anchor of hope for our souls. Unlike a sailor at sea, we have an anchor that isn't at the bottom of the ocean. The image of an anchor depicted in Hebrews is an anchor that is hurled amid the stormy seas and wild winds of our lives on earth up into heaven, where it is fastened to the very throne of God. Our lives are anchored in heaven!

Even though the believer's life is anchored in Christ, there are times when an honest picture of our life might appropriately be titled "Struggling on Stormy Seas." At times like these we fight to keep our head above water, and we identify with Emil Brunner, who said, "What oxygen is for the lungs, such is hope for the meaning of human life." It's through these struggles that we grow in hope, and when we're honest about our neediness, we're prompted to look for hope. In addressing our struggle to hope, honesty is an appropriate place to begin.

Honesty — Prelude to Hope

One of our friends, a college professor, enjoys telling of a time he wasn't completely candid with his students. Early in one class session he demonstrated an equation on the overhead projector. When he'd completed his demonstration, he turned off the projector switch and yanked the power cord out of the wall socket—and the cord snapped back and the plug hit him on the nose.

Although his nose hurt a lot, his pride hurt even worse. Groping for something to say, he blurted out, "Didn't hurt!"

The professor tried to go on teaching and act as though he was fine, but he soon noticed that his students were snickering. Although he hadn't admitted his pain, it was impossible for him to cover up the blood that was trickling down his face.

Sometimes we treat the deep pain of our lives in much the same way. Even though we are in debilitating pain, we try to ignore it and pretend that we're fine. Not being honest with ourselves, we lose credibility with those around us. We also deprive them of the privilege of coming alongside us. Contrary to what some of us think or how some of us were raised, admitting pain is not a sign of weakness. It's a sign of integrity.

How can we ever find hope if we're not first honest about our pain to God, to ourselves and to others? No matter what kind of loss we're dealing with, acknowledging our pain is a healthy place to begin. Consider some of the honest feelings penned by some of the psalmists:

> I am worn out from groaning;
>> all night long I flood my bed with weeping
>> and drench my couch with tears. (Psalm 6:6)

> Why, O LORD, do you stand far off?
>> Why do you hide yourself in times of trouble? (Psalm 10:1)

Think also of Mary and Martha's honesty. After their brother Lazarus died, they each said to Jesus, one at a time, "If you had been here, my brother would not have died" (John 11:21, 32).

We may never understand what God has allowed to happen in our life or in the lives of people around us. Asking questions of God is part of an honest, childlike faith, even though we may not receive complete answers until we see him face to face. Philip Yancey says there are three questions that no one asks out loud: Is God unfair? Is God silent? Is God hidden?[1] Even Jesus, as he hung on the cross, cried out, "My God, my God, why have you forsaken me?" (Matthew 27:46). At that darkest—and brightest—moment of history, when Jesus took our sin upon himself, he felt forsaken and he was honest about it. Following his example, we can learn to be honest with him, with ourselves and with others. It's a practice of integrity that leads to hope and healing.

Whether our loss involves cancer, a job, a death, a disability or a marital crisis, our grief needs to be acknowledged honestly. How we grieve is influenced by a number of factors, including our personality, the intensity and timing of the loss, and whether or not our loss was anticipated. Although no two people grieve exactly the same way, the process does tend to follow a pattern. Elisabeth Kübler-Ross described the stages of loss as shock or denial, anger, bargaining for more time, depression and acceptance.[2] Amy Carmichael understood the goal of the last stage when she said, "In acceptance lieth peace."[3]

Working through any significant loss or disappointment takes time. Even as healing is occurring, "surges of sorrow" may be triggered at the least expected moments and bring a flood of emotions. As we move through the stages, we discover that we wake up some mornings feeling encouraged that our loss is no longer the first thought of each day. That's progress.

As difficult as the grief process may feel, it's necessary to deal with it honestly. "Unless the grief process is confronted courageously, you won't arrive at a healthy resolution and be able to move on. If you don't address grief directly, you run the risk of getting stuck in your grief for a long time."[4] Even when we're grieving, we need enough to go around in other areas of life. Getting stuck in our grief consumes the emotional energy we need to keep going.

People who face fresh grief with unfinished business from some other loss discover their grief to be greatly compounded. If a husband dies and his wife isn't on speaking terms with her in-laws, you can imagine the extra turmoil that affects everyone in the family. That's another reason for us to keep short accounts with God and each other in the present. "If it is possible, as far as it depends on you, live at peace with everyone" (Romans 12:18).

Obedience Fosters Hope

Two weeks before I (Ellen) attended a convention in Atlanta with my husband, we were watching the evening news. An announcer came on to report that the parking lot of a large Atlanta hotel, built on the side of a hill, had collapsed into a sinkhole. As the TV camera zoomed in to show a picture of the collapse, Jim exclaimed, "That's the hotel we're supposed to stay in!"

The hotel administrators kindly made reservations elsewhere for us, but the damage to the property was substantial, both physical damage and lost revenue. After a series of storms had pounded the area, it became evident that the foundation under the lot had been washed away in the rush of an underground stream.

Collapses in our lives can be similarly devastating, especially if we've built on a shifting foundation. The foundation of a Christ-follower's life is obedience to Christ. Storms will inevitably come to all of our lives—it's a matter of when, not if. If we live in a pattern of obedience to Christ, we learn that even in a storm our foundation is the Rock. Our hope is kept alive, and our character is strengthened rather than weakened.

> *I desire not only to call you "Lord" but to do what you say. By your grace I will come to you, hear your words and put them into practice. Then I will be like one who built a house, who dug down deep and laid the foundation on rock, and when a flood came, the torrent struck that house but could not shake it, because it was well built.*
> See LUKE 6:46-48

When storms in our life result from our disobedience, though, those storms sometimes plunge us into a sinkhole and take our hopes right along with them. Sudden tragedies do not give us time to begin building a solid foundation, but they do have a way of revealing how we've built.

Although disobedience and poor choices do sabotage hope, we need to be careful not to assume that all sufferings or heartaches are the result of specific sins. People who attempt to interpret all pain through that grid will complicate their grief with guilt. Job, a godly man who endured great suffering, was "blameless and upright; he feared God and shunned evil" (Job 1:1). All the way through the Bible, men and women who trust and obey God are blessed. Even when they go through suffering, their obedience produces blessing and hope.

Perspective Sustains Hope

A teacher assigned to visit children in a large city hospital received a routine call requesting that she visit a particular child. She took the boy's name and room number and was told by the teacher on the other end of the line, "We're studying nouns and adverbs in his class now. I'd be grateful if you could help him with his homework so he doesn't fall behind the others."

When the visiting teacher came to the boy's room, she realized it was located in the hospital's burn unit. No one had prepared her to find a young boy horribly burned and in great pain. She couldn't just turn and walk out, so she awkwardly stammered, "I'm the hospital teacher, and your teacher sent me to help you with nouns and adverbs."

The next morning a nurse on the burn unit asked her, "What did you do to that boy?" Before she could finish a profusion of apologies, the nurse interrupted her: "You don't understand. We've been very worried about him, but ever since you were here yesterday, his whole attitude has changed. He's fighting back, responding to treatment. . . . It's as though he's decided to live."

The boy later explained that he had completely given up hope until he saw that teacher. Everything changed when he came to a simple realization. With joyful tears, he expressed it this way: "They wouldn't send a teacher to work on nouns and adverbs with a dying boy, would they?"[5]

At times we feel a lot like that young boy. Life seems so painful and so difficult. We're not sure we have much to live for, and we wonder if it's really worth the effort to keep going. But then we learn—or we remember—that God did much more than send us a teacher. He sent his Son to die for us because he loves us. And if we ask him, he forgives us, stays with us, helps us and one day brings us to live with him forever. Our perspective—our mental outlook—changes. We begin to realize what's most important in life. Someone who has guided us in the past and has eyes to see the future tells us we can trust him. He not only sees the future but controls it.

We're able to live with a hopeful perspective when we understand the character of God, remember his faithfulness in the past and look ahead with anticipation for what he's promised us in the future.

Knowing God's character. In order to understand people, we watch what they do and observe how they act. It's no different with God. When we open the Old Testament we learn a lot about who God is. He created the earth and filled it with life. He held back the waters of the Red Sea for the Israelites escaping slavery. He provided manna and quail for them to eat in the wilderness. He kept his promises. He remembered Hannah and opened her womb. He protected Daniel in the lion's den. And he heard Jonah's prayer from the belly of a fish.

When we open the New Testament, we discover more about Jesus—God with us. He taught with authority. He reached out his hands and healed lepers. He forgave sins. He blessed the poor, the hungry, the mourners and the persecuted. He was full of grace and truth. He calmed the storm. He gathered children into his arms. He sought out sinners. He suffered and died for us. He conquered death for us. And he's preparing heaven for us.

Seeing God's activity and faithfulness in the past is a prelude to knowing him personally—not as a distant God but as our dearest Father and closest friend. As we talk to him and place our trust in him, we discover that the God who walked through the furnace with Shadrach, Meshach and Abednego is the same God who walks with us today in each of our fiery trials. We realize that God is good, he is in control and he makes no mistakes. Understanding the character of God transforms our perspective on all of life—especially our perspective on disappointment and loss.

Remembering God's faithfulness. When Moses was on top of Mount Sinai receiving the Ten Commandments from God, the people he was leading (who were supposed to be waiting for him at the bottom of the mountain) forgot God and lost all perspective. Because they thought God's calendar wasn't moving along quickly enough, they created an idol in the form of a golden calf. Fashioning the idol was bad enough, but the Hebrew people proceeded to add to their idol worship all kinds of pagan revelry and immorality.

Their loss of perspective caused them to lose much more than their perspective. At least twenty-three thousand lives were lost.

If these people had looked to the past, what would they have seen? They would have remembered how God had caused water to spring forth from a rock. They would have remembered how God had provided quail and manna in the desert. They would have remembered the Passover, the night the angel of death had passed over their houses and spared the lives of their firstborn sons. If they had looked back, they would have remembered God's faithfulness.

> *For great is his love toward us, and the faithfulness of the LORD endures forever.*
> PSALM 117:2

One of the advantages of having lived awhile is that we can remember what God has done over time in our lives. Viewing our life retrospectively, we have an increased appreciation for God's timing, and we can often see how previous experiences were essential preparation for what followed. God's delays are not always denials. Sometimes we sincerely thank God that he didn't grant all of our wishes and requests. We may be like six-year-old Ashley, who threw a tantrum in Kmart because her mother wouldn't buy a Barbie doll for her, not realizing that an American Girl baby doll was wrapped and waiting under the Christmas tree!

Joseph, an Old Testament character, experienced many painful delays. Dropped into a pit by his brothers, all he could do was pray. Falsely accused by Potiphar's wife, he must have ached to be vindicated. Feeling forgotten in prison, Joseph remained faithful to God. Eventually he was chosen to become second in command to Pharaoh, and through Joseph the whole Hebrew nation was preserved. As Joseph stood before Pharaoh and received his high position, can you imagine what must have been going through his mind? "Joseph would always remember how he was lifted out of that pit. He knew God was with him. He had seen God act, and he could never forget that."[6]

Joseph later stated to his brothers that what they had intended for harm, God meant for good (Genesis 50:20). His statement was full of honesty, obedience and perspective. That kind of hope is what has sustained people in disappointment and loss throughout the ages. It sustained holocaust survivors. It sustained prisoners of war. It is the source of serenity for any of us today who are experiencing difficult circumstances and relationships.

Looking to the future. Having worked as an emergency room nurse for several years, I (Joan) am convinced that Christians die better. They don't die hoping that they'll go to heaven—

they die knowing. Although family members left behind after a death still have to deal with grief and loss, hope puts their loss into perspective.

Establishing a relationship with God through faith encourages the perspective that our brief life here on earth is a preamble to eternal life. We look forward to seeing God and spending eternity with him in heaven, where there is no more death, mourning, crying or pain (Revelation 21:4). Because of God's presence in our life, we're learning to accept the heartaches of the here and now as temporary, realizing that they help prepare us to go and live with God. "Our citizenship is in heaven. And we eagerly await a Savior from there, the Lord Jesus Christ" (Philippians 3:20).

> *We do not want you to be misinformed, brothers and sisters, about those who have died, so that you may not grieve as others do who have no hope.*
> 1 THESSALONIANS 4:13 (NRSV)

Peter Marshall knew a mother whose son was critically ill, facing death. The mother had spent hours nursing him and playing with him, knowing that the boy's days on earth were short. One day the boy asked his mother what it would be like to die. After the mother sent up a quick prayer for wisdom and composure, she said,

> "Kenneth, do you remember when you were a tiny boy how you used to play so hard all day that when night came you were too tired even to undress and you'd tumble into your mother's bed and fall asleep? That was not your bed, it was not where you belonged. You would only stay there a little while. Much to your surprise you would wake up and find yourself in your own bed in your own room. You were there because someone had loved you and taken care of you. Your father had come with big strong arms and carried you away. Kenneth, darling, death is just like that. We wake up some morning to find ourselves in the other

room. Our room where we belong, because the Lord Jesus loved us and died for us."

The lad's shining face looking up into hers told her that the point had gone home and there would be no more fear, only love and trust in his little heart as he went to meet the Father in heaven. He never questioned again. Several weeks later, he fell asleep just as she had said, and his Father's big, strong arms carried him to his own room.[7]

This mother, like Moses' mother, had her eyes fixed on God. Just as Moses' mother, Jochebed, hoped and waited for God's intervention while her baby floated down the river in a little basket, her grown son later hoped and waited for God during Egyptian captivity and wilderness wanderings. Hebrews 11:27 tells us that Moses "persevered because he saw him who is invisible." He waited with his eyes fixed on God.

All throughout Scripture hope forms a couplet with waiting on God. Hope and waiting go hand in hand. Every time we have to wait, we're presented with yet another opportunity to hope in God—another opportunity to see him who is invisible.

What are you waiting for today? Are you waiting for your husband to find a job? Are you waiting for a prodigal child to return? Are you waiting for money to pay your medical bills? Are you waiting for your husband to desire a vital and growing relationship with you? We wait with hope as we focus our eyes on him who is invisible. It's part of living with an eternal perspective.

Encouragement Brings Hope

As C. S. Lewis notes, it's often our pain that prompts us to pray. "God whispers to us in our pleasures, speaks in our conscience, but shouts in our pain. Pain is God's megaphone to rouse a deaf world."[8] It was pain in the childhood of James Dobson's wife, Shirley, that prompted her to pray, and God's response to her prayers brought encouragement.

> My wife, Shirley, did not grow up in a Christian home, and her experiences were very different from mine. Her father was an alcoholic who abused his family and spoke of God only when cursing. Shirley's mother, while not a Christian, was a wonderful woman who loved her two children. She recognized her need for assistance in raising her kids and began sending them to a neighborhood evangelical church when they were very young. There, Shirley learned about Jesus—and she learned to pray.
>
> This little girl, trapped in poverty and the heartache of alcoholism, began talking to the Lord about her family. Especially after her parents were divorced, she asked Him to grant two requests. First, she prayed for a Christian stepfather who would love and provide for them. Second, Shirley knew she wanted to have a godly home and family someday. She began asking the Lord for a Christian husband when the time came to marry. It touches my heart today to think about that child, alone on her knees in her bedroom, talking to God about her need. I was out there somewhere oblivious of her existence, but the Lord had me in a long-term training program. By the time I met this pretty young lady in college, I did not have to be pushed.
>
> That story beautifully illustrates the efficacy of prayer. The great God of the universe, with all His majesty and power, was not too busy to hear the small voice of a child in need. He not only brought the two of us together, but He sent a fine, never-married man to be Shirley's new stepfather. Both her parents are Christians today and are serving the Lord in their community.[9]

It's important to be thankful when we receive what we asked for, but how do we respond when that doesn't happen? It's easy to assume that if our prayers aren't answered the way we had hoped, it must be due to our lack of faith. Thinking that way would only compound our suffering and reduce God to someone we think we could control if we just mustered up enough faith. After seeing that "all the ways of the LORD are loving and faithful" (Psalm 25:10), it would be a "trivialization of God" to mistake our agenda for his and try to write his job description for him.[10] May God's Spirit give us faith to continue to hope in God even when we don't receive what we asked, so that we can say with Job, "Though he slay me, yet will I hope in him" (Job 13:15).

> *For everything that was written in the past was written to teach us, so that through endurance and the encouragement of the Scriptures we might have hope.*
> ROMANS 15:4

Another way we are encouraged to hope in God is through his Word. One of our friends shares in her own words how God's Word has encouraged her to hope in the midst of a difficult marriage.

For many years, I felt like a victim in my marriage. It seemed that most of my trials were related to my husband's emotional and psychological problems, and that there was no way out for me. I often fell into the habit of feeling sorry for myself and even envying other people's family life. The "me as a victim" mindset kept me believing I just had to endure all these trials because I was married to this man. I was not only a victim, but I had also become a martyr. I thought only about my problems, and never about what God wanted to teach me.

As I began to dig deep into the Scriptures, God's Spirit taught me how wrong I was to think this way. My Heavenly Father's plan is always for my good, and these trials were allowed in my life to mold me and change my character into the image of Christ. How often I viewed my circumstances only in terms of pain and suffering, but God saw that they were accomplishing what he desired, fitted together perfectly into his plans for eternity.

My focus began to change from the circumstances themselves to the truths God wanted to teach me about himself and our relationship. He is allowing me to go through these earthly trials so that I will grow up in my faith and become a mature child of God. I now see that this life on earth is so much more than all these trials; it is preparing me for what is to come. His Word says, "And this small and temporary trouble we suffer will bring us a tremendous and eternal glory, much greater than the trouble. For we fix our attention not on things that are seen, but on things that are unseen. What can be seen lasts only for a time, but what cannot be seen lasts forever" (2 Corinthians 4:17-18 TEV).

God also uses other believers to encourage and inspire us to hope. I (Ellen) remember a season in my life that felt hopeless. I couldn't imagine how anything good could ever come out of the painful circumstances I was experiencing.

One of my friends bought me a framed plaque that displayed Romans 15:13 in beautiful calligraphy: "May the God of hope fill you with all joy and peace as you trust in him." As much as I appreciated my friend's kindness, I struggled to believe the verse for myself. So I set the plaque face down on a bedroom table. Every now and then I'd dust it off and put it back on the table, face down.

But after several months, the verse that my friend was praying for me began to spark a flicker of hope in my heart, and eventually I began praying it too. Before long, that prayer became a reality, and I propped up the plaque, displaying it in a place where I could view it frequently. It's been standing up properly ever since. Sometimes God uses our friends to encourage us toward hope when we feel utterly depleted.

After World War II, German students volunteered to help rebuild a cathedral in England, one of many casualties of the Luftwaffe bombings. As the work progressed, debate broke out on how to best restore a large statue of Jesus with His arms out-stretched and bearing the familiar inscription, "Come unto Me." Careful patching could repair all damage to the statue except for Christ's hands, which had been destroyed by bomb fragments. Should they attempt the delicate task of reshaping those hands? Finally the workers reached a decision that still stands today. The statue of Jesus had no hands, and the inscription now reads, "Christ has no hands but ours."[11]

Through Christ's power, we can help to bring encouragement to seemingly hopeless situations all around us.

Is There Enough Hope to Go Around?

Joseph Bayly, a man who experienced the death of three of his children, wrote,

> Our peace is not in understanding everything that happens to us and our children but in knowing that He is in control of sickness and health and even death. We accept life's mysteries and suffering unexplained because they are known to God and we know Him. . . . We believe that God is love. He is kind. . . . He does not lightly afflict the children of men. I cannot explain it, but my wife and I have never been more convinced of His love for us and our children than when we have turned from a fresh grave.[12]

If disappointment and loss are inescapable components of our lives, then how can we make sure that our suffering is not wasted? How can we make sure that our suffering produces the perseverance, character and hope of Romans 5:2-5? Even though we can't always choose our circumstances, we can choose our response to those circumstances. And our response, to a large extent, determines whether we will become *bitter* people or *better* people.

Honesty, Obedience, Perspective and Encouragement all point us to Christ, the secure anchor of hope. He is the One who sustains us when it feels like there just isn't enough hope to go around. If we allow God to work through the disappointments and losses of our lives, our sufferings will not be wasted. Rather, we'll know more of God's presence, we'll become more understanding of the pain of others, and we'll grow more hopeful of the joys of spending eternity with him. Then we can echo the words of Bishop Handley Moule: "There is no situation so chaotic that God cannot, from that situation, create something that is surpassingly good. He did it at Creation. He did it at the cross. He is doing it today."[13]

> *Christians are people of hope and not despair. Because we know that God, who had the first word, will have the last. He is never thwarted or caught napping by the circumstances of our lives. To have faith in Jesus does not mean we try to pretend that bad things are really good. Rather we know that God will take our difficulties and weave them into purposes we cannot see as yet.*
> REBECCA MANLEY PIPPERT

Reflection Questions

1. State one reason it's difficult for us to be honest about our feelings.

2. What is one way we might be helpful to a friend or relative who is grieving?

3. What does obedience have to do with hope? Read Luke 6:46-48; Titus 2:11-14; Jude 20-21.

4. Read Exodus 32:1-8. How had the Israelites lost perspective? How do we sometimes lose perspective?

5. Read Genesis 50:15-21. What enabled Joseph to become better and not bitter?

6. Read Hebrews 11:13-16, 24-29. How did Moses persevere through his hardships?

7. Read Isaiah 53:3-12. Why do you think Jesus understands our sufferings?

8. What is one time you have been encouraged through prayer? God's Word? other Christ-followers?

9

Here and Now Is Just One Season of Life

There is a time for everything,
and a season for every activity under heaven.

ECCLESIASTES 3:1

*M*y (Joan's) favorite season of the year is autumn. I can't resist picking up brilliant red and gold leaves, which often find their way into dictionaries, Bibles, hymnbooks or letters to friends. My husband, Jim, teases me for exclaiming each year, "This is the most beautiful fall I can remember!" While the turkey roasts on Thanksgiving Day we take our traditional family hike on the Illinois Prairie Path, sometimes accompanied by the first snowflakes of the season.

My (Ellen's) favorite season is spring. My family tolerates each long Chicago winter as we anticipate our annual trip to Florida over spring break. When we return, it's almost time to plant five flats of multicolored impatiens along the north side of our home. As the thermometer marker outside our backdoor rises, I am delighted to exchange my fleece, headband and gloves for shorts and a T-shirt when I take my daily walk.

What is your favorite season? Because seasons remind us of predictable sequences, we tend to plan our life around them. We buy flowerpots in spring, swimsuits before summer, school supplies for fall and Christmas gifts before winter. In the same way that the seasons of nature are divinely ordered by God, so are the seasons of our lives. Because God is the only One who knows the end from the beginning, it is through knowing him that we can discover meaning and fulfillment in each season of life. "One can come to know God through the docile learning of childhood, in the midst of the full activity of maturity, or in the contemplative age of retirement. It is this knowing which remains as the common denominator of all life's stages."[1]

No matter what season of life we're in now, it's helpful for us to understand them all. Just as it's helpful for a student to obtain a syllabus at the beginning of a semester indicating what to expect in the months to come, it's helpful for each of us to know what to expect in the coming seasons. Reflecting on the seasons past and anticipating the seasons yet to come gives us valuable perspective on the big picture of life. As we make some sense of our history and formulate realistic goals for our future, we're better equipped to make intentional choices and decisions in each season of life, influencing whether or not we'll have enough to go around both now and in the future. What are some of the challenges of each season, and how can we meet them?

Spring

Lilacs budding, breezes blowing, raindrops falling—it's spring! Full of fragrance, color and warmth, spring is a time that awakens our senses to the world around us. The springtime of a woman's life is much the same. Seeds of crops yet to be harvested are being planted, and a young woman's senses are awakening to a variety of relationships. "This season is characterized by conscious plans, choices, and commitments within the context of dreams and goals, which tend to be primarily relational."[2]

Renegotiating relationships with original family. One of the first tasks of springtime for any young woman is renegotiating relationships with her family of origin, often prompted by her going off to college or moving into her own apartment. A healthy family understands the young woman's need to branch out, and they facilitate this process by encouraging her, whereas a troubled family will tend to make her life difficult by clinging to her or attempting to control her. Leaving a single-parent family can be more complicated, especially if the child has been a main source of companionship and emotional support. Optimally, each young person's step in coming of age is characterized by decreasing financial dependence and increasing confidence and autonomy. "Indeed, childhood is chiefly preparation for the all important event of leaving home."[3]

Some young adults in the springtime of life feel that they have begun to outgrow their parents intellectually, emotionally and spiritually. This was true for Kristin, the first child in her farm family to pursue higher education. When Kristin's parents visited her at college, she was ashamed for feeling embarrassed that her parents didn't appear as sophisticated as some of the other parents. As she matured, though, she developed an appreciation for her parents' hard work and financial sacrifice that had enabled her to grow. Like all young adults, Kristin was sorting out which patterns from her family she wanted to continue and which she wanted to change. Her parents were wise not to take this too personally, realizing that it was all part of growing up. Isn't it amazing that as youth mature, they are often impressed with how much more intelligent their parents have become?

Although young adults are less dependent on their parents at this stage, if parents have "left the lights on" children will come back to the secure base for reassurance when they need it. We have both received late-night phone calls from our young adult children, hearing on the other end of the line, "Something's troubling me—do you have a few minutes to talk?" If during the childhood years children have been raised to trust their parents, talk to their parents and grow confident in who God made them to be, their adult relationships with their parents will likely be rich.

Establishing meaningful friendships. Another important task for the woman in the springtime of her life is establishing meaningful friendships. Young women begin to learn many lessons in the laboratory of maturing friendship, where responsibility, accountability and unselfishness come into play. As painful as roommate squabbles or broken dating relationships can be, they provide opportunities for growth in communication and character.

Parents and mentors can be valuable sources of wisdom and balance during these challenging times in a young person's relationships. Even if parents are out of the loop in a young person's friendships, they can pray for their child's friends, professors, bosses and roommates as well as show hospitality whenever possible. I (Ellen) still enjoy baking for my young adult sons and their friends—they don't relish a plate of cookies any less now than they did when they were in first grade.

"After I graduated from college and moved into an apartment," says Tiffany, "I started hitting the snooze button on my alarm and drifting back to sleep on Sunday mornings. Unfortunately, other things began drifting too—like my friendships and my outlook on life. When I decided to find a local church community, I quickly welcomed the benefits of the instruction and support that I received. I felt like a lonely sheep who was happy to return to the flock." The springtime of life can be lonely for a young person who has moved away from home, especially if she's missing the friends, fun and fellowship of her college days. Connecting with a local church community helps her with all those needs—and a whole lot more.

Making career decisions. The springtime of life also includes vocational choices and career decisions. College students are choosing their course of study, while others are seeking work in an area that interests them. Parents and mentors can be immensely helpful to young women who are wading through the complexity of career options that our rapidly changing world offers us. Answers to these questions do not always come quickly, so the young woman who has older adults who are willing to spend time listening, caring and sorting through these challenges is blessed indeed.

Nancy Lewis, director of career services at Wheaton College, enjoys helping students discover their areas of natural giftedness by looking at what motivates them. She observes that although many college students are initially hesitant to face career issues, they often find computer assessments to be a nonthreatening way to begin. After a student's personality, values, natural abilities and interests have been assessed, Nancy helps the student prepare a resumé, look for internships and schedule informational interviews. Most colleges offer these valuable services for students who otherwise might not know where to begin.

My (Joan's) father, Paul Bartel, reminded me that if I loved God with all my heart, any vocation would become Christian service. God has designed all of us uniquely, so whether our career involves engineering, homemaking, medicine, teaching or music, we can each use our gifts to the glory of God. "And whatever you do, whether in word or deed, do it all in the name of the Lord Jesus, giving thanks to God the Father through him" (Colossians 3:17).

Preparing for marriage. For some young women, the springtime of life includes marriage. Kayla recently began planning her wedding and is immersed in decisions about dresses, attendants, churches, invitations, flowers and more. She and her future husband, Brian, are also entering into new relationships with each other's family. They have a lot of questions facing them, like, Where and how will we celebrate the holidays? Will we be vegetarians like Kayla's family, or will we eat whatever we want like Brian's family? Will we attend Brian's parents' church, Kayla's parents' church or a new church altogether?

Amid all the questions and decisions of planning and executing a marriage, premarital counseling and young-married Sunday school classes are tremendously helpful to young couples today. Interacting with other newlyweds and older role models is a huge encouragement at a time when they're working to build a solid foundation for the years to come.

Seeds that are sown in the springtime of a young woman's life help determine the kinds of crops she will reap in later seasons. How a young woman renegotiates with her original family, establishes friendships, chooses a career and approaches marriage influences how much she'll have to go around in future seasons.

Summer

Running barefoot in the grass, picking corn and building lemonade stands—whether we're planning a trip to the beach, going to a ball game or taking kids on a picnic, summer is a time of adventure. Falling between young adulthood and midlife—the thirtysomething years—the summertime of our life is adventurous as well. Our adventures may include being single and doing extra traveling, raising a family with our husband, investing in the lives of our children, establishing new friendships or becoming involved at church or school. All of these adventures need to be planned carefully and intentionally, because successful adventures always begin with wise choices.

The summer season of our life—sometimes called the deadline decade—presents us with many choices. How many children will we have? How will we raise them? When do we begin saving for our children's education? Should we go back to work? During this season a single woman may be affirming or accepting her singleness. The young mother may begin to experience the tug of multiple phone calls begging her to be involved in PTA, Sunday school or soccer tournaments. When her children start school, she may begin to wonder if there's enough of her to go around to return to some academic pursuits or employment. Or a married career woman may be opting for "last-chance children" before her biological clock runs out. These complex choices are highly personal and are contingent on our circumstances and resources. Single mothers may not have the same options, but they certainly deserve the understanding and support of those who do. The choices we make in this season have huge implications for the years to come.

Words that Moses spoke to the Israelites, recorded in Deuteronomy 30:19-20, are poignant as we consider the choices we make in the summer of our life: "I have set before you life and death, blessings and curses. Now choose life, so that you and your children may live and that you may love the LORD your

God, listen to his voice, and hold fast to him." *That's* the most important choice, influencing every other decision.

Young women who marry and begin a family are bombarded with daily decisions about whose needs to address first. They are required to make enormous adjustments in their lifestyle, employment and sleep patterns (or lack thereof!), and to develop new levels of selflessness. The years of parenting toddlers may be the epitome of not having enough to go around. In the interest of making good choices, this may be a good time to reevaluate what you could let go for a while. Keep in mind that a young mother needs to maintain some outside activities, lest her world shrink to Pampers and pacifiers. At the same time, from our perspective the preschool years seem so fleeting and yet so developmentally crucial that we're convinced you'll never regret spending too much time with your children.

As wonderful as it is for young moms to be home with their kids, they do need occasional diversions to help them fully appreciate their roles, be more effective and keep their sanity. I (Joan) recall the day my eighteen-month-old son Winsor put our kitten in the refrigerator, drank from the aquarium, put orange juice in the steam iron and fingerpainted with chocolate syrup. That's a day I chose to have a time out.

As children grow and are involved in more and more activities, moms are typically faced (bombarded?) with increasing choices about how and where they will volunteer their time. Through some trial and error, I (Joan) settled on a formula that included one commitment (only!) to each of three extrafamilial activities at any point:

☐ one community agency—the hospital auxiliary was my choice because my husband was a physician on the staff

☐ the school my children attended—this involved, at various times, being room mother (once for each child), being a PTA officer, helping with the volunteer art history program (as "picture lady"), and during high school years being on the Parent Advisory Council

☐ church—usually a responsibility relating to the activities my children were involved in, like Sunday school teacher or youth group sponsor

At a high school reunion during the summertime of life, I (Ellen) observed the results of choices some of my former classmates had made. Some were single, some were married with children ranging from tots to teens, and some were divorced. Some were raising children wisely; others had family stories that unfolded like nightmares. Some women had children and husbands who appeared to treat them with respect; others had children and husbands who seemed to treat them more like doormats. Some classmates had been saving their money and investing it slowly but surely; others seemed to be up to their eyeballs in debt. Some talked mostly about money, jobs and houses; others talked about things that last, like God's goodness and presence in their lives. Interacting with former classmates at that reunion reminded me that the choices we make during the summer of our life have great significance and lasting consequences.

Autumn

Watching birds fly south, walking through rustling leaves, carving pumpkins and baking apple crisp—autumn is a season of transitions. We put away our sundresses and unpack our wool sweaters. We shut down the air conditioner and fire up the furnace. Autumn is also a time for serving. We offer thanks for food grown during the summer and serve Thanksgiving dinner with all the trimmings.

The season of autumn in a woman's life is like that. We experience transitions in our roles and relationships, while we serve others out of the overflow of God's goodness to us. Let's look at several of the transitions we are likely to face.

New roles. It is not unusual for a woman in this season to take on the role of "kin-keeper," "dispatcher" or "control central" for both kids *and* parents. My (Ellen's) husband, Jim, and I began to experience this transition during the years I was working on this book. Following our son Chad's college graduation, we helped him move into his first apartment. Some months later we helped Jim's parents move into an assisted living center. We began to feel needed by both the older generation and the younger generation. These midlife years are sometimes described as the "sandwich years," when we're "caught between aging parents who suddenly need help and children who are breaking away . . . like butter between two slices of bread."[4] Elderly parents may need guidance, support or a place to live, and they often depend on their midlife children for companionship and consultation. Midlife women sometimes begin to feel as if they are parenting their parents and their kids at the same time!

As hard as it is for some of us to see our children move out, that's what we're preparing them for, and we're faced with new challenges if they don't. "In a recent study of three generation families, it was noted that the failure of a young adult to leave home at the expected or anticipated time increases strain and conflict among parents and their young adult children."[5] I (Joan) treasure the calligraphy framed in dried flowers that Jeanne made for me when she became engaged to my son Winsor: "There are two things you give your children. One is roots—the other is wings." (The calligraphy still hangs in my family room, but I insist it wasn't an even swap—a wall hanging in exchange for a son!)

A phone call I (Joan) received on the morning of one Christmas Eve illustrates some of the normal feelings women experience during the years their children are leaving the nest. A dear friend who has many family members and friends called to say, "I just wanted to chat with a friend. My husband and I are orphans, none of our children are in town, and we're not needed this Christmas." She didn't need to remind me that both she and her husband had recently lost their parents. And although she and her husband had volunteered to work in a homeless shelter, they were told they were not needed! This was not the Christmas they had anticipated. Being resilient people, this couple decided to drop in on a few relatives and friends to wish them a merry Christmas. It wasn't what they would have planned, but they now have a story to share with younger generations who gather around their tree in coming years.

Surviving retirement. Another transition some women face in the autumn of life is retirement, or watching their husband deal with a career crisis or early retirement. A woman may feel that her turf has been invaded; she may have trouble adjusting to having an escort to the grocery store. If her husband spends a lot of time in the house, her friends may not feel free to drop in for coffee or lunch.

Hopefully a woman in this situation will continue to practice the communication skills she's developed through the years and talk openly and honestly with her husband about her feelings. Together they can develop boundaries and routines that will respect the needs of them both at this stage of life.

Is depression inevitable? I (Joan) work with quite a few midlife women who suffer from depression during the transitions of this season. Many of these women have been very giving—maybe too giving—and have not expected their families and friends to treat them with respect and appreciation. Hence I have coined the term "doormat depression." Some women have confused the idea of being a servant (as taught in Matthew 20:26) with being a doormat. If they put up with disrespectful treatment, only retreating to their bedroom in tears like a martyr, they may receive more of the same treatment in the future.

In her book *Seasons* Anita Spencer comments that women come into the season of autumn full of empathy, sensitivity and adaptability but that they are wise to add the qualities of independence, confidence and initiative for the years to come.[6] Any woman who enters this season feeling unappreciated and devalued will have an even bigger challenge dealing with the changing hormones and swinging moods of menopause. Women who enter this season with renewed confidence and purpose, though, are more likely to avoid unwanted depression during the autumn season.

Service. Service—the healthy kind, not the doormat kind—is another important aspect of the autumn season of a woman's life. In order for a woman to be fulfilled during this stage, she needs to invest her energy in other people. If she chooses to be self-absorbed, she becomes dull, inactive or depressed. One of the ways that women in the autumn of life can resist stagnation and self-indulgence is to make valuable contributions in the lives of the younger generation.

> *People who don't develop a life of service begin to indulge themselves as if they were their one and only child.*
> EUGENE WRIGHT

As grandchildren arrive, they introduce new possibilities for us to be involved in the lives of young people. Many grandparents attest to the joys of loving and nurturing the next generation without feeling total responsibility for the outcome. "If Mommy says no, ask Grandma" becomes the password. Judith Viorst sees grandchildren as a gift that young parents give to their parents.[7] I (Ellen) like to turn that thought around—grandparents are gifts parents give to their kids—to describe how I feel about my parents. Not only have they babysat, baked cookies, invited our kids for overnights, taken them to Florida and toured Europe with them, but they have also given our children the wonderful gift of two godly examples and lots of prayer.

> *A harmonious intimacy between grandparents and grandchildren can very often be an incomparably precious blessing for both.*
> PAUL TOURNIER

My (Joan's) friend Esther, an active grandmother, has suggested, "If you don't have young children in your circle of family or friends, seek some out in order to keep a sense of awe and wonder in your life." There is great mutual benefit in adopting "grandchildren," especially in our mobile and fragmented society where extended families may be widely separated.

Fulfillment in this season of our life not only comes through investing ourselves in family members but involves people in a vast array of settings. Perhaps that's why Erik Erikson described the central choice in this stage of life as the choice between stagnation and generativity. I (Joan) believed that teaching college students was a wonderful way to resist stagnation; I often exclaimed, "They are the hope of the world!" I insist that they taught me more than I taught them. Investing in mentoring relationships, tutoring or volunteering in pediatric wards of hospitals will bring similar rewards.

Phil and Carla model for us what a meaningful and fulfilling season of life the autumn can be. After being employed as a high school principal for many years, Phil retired early because of an attractive early-retirement package. Carla left her position of school nurse soon afterward. Phil now uses his education and experiences to teach an occasional education course at one local college and supervise student teachers at another. He also donates about twenty hours a week as chair of the board of missions at a large church. Maintaining contact with hundreds of missionaries around the world, he has even made trips to visit some of them. In addition, he serves on the board of a local agency that serves at-risk families and youth. Carla works in a resale shop that benefits the same agency, as well as serving at church. A typical "sandwich generation" woman, she stops by almost daily to visit her 101-year-old father in a retirement center.

Together, Carla and Phil give support and encouragement to their children as they parent the next generation. Their grandchildren are often seen with Phil and Carla as they go about their many "random acts of kindness," and a precious granddaughter with special needs is often an integral member of their team. A delightful sense of humor is the icing on the cake for this couple, who give a living demonstration of service in the autumn season of their lives.

> We are not called to live here and survive. We are called to live here and change our world.
> CLIVE CALVER

Carla and Phil's life theme is Psalm 48:14: "For this God is our God forever and ever; he will be our guide even to the end."

Grateful for what God has done for us, we can be intentional about serving in fulfilling endeavors and experience the enduring joys of giving to others. If we don't invest in the lives of others, our hearts will shrivel up, and we won't have enough compassion to go around. In the feeding of the five thousand, remember, there wasn't enough food until it began to be given away. "It is possible to give freely and become more wealthy, but those who are stingy will lose everything. The generous prosper and are satisfied; those who refresh others will themselves be refreshed" (Proverbs 11:24-25 NLT).

Winter

Warming by the fire, celebrating Christmas traditions, slowing down. As bare trees outside our windows remind us of leaves that have fallen, we also look ahead to signs of new life in the spring. We're reminded of nature's cycle of life to death to life. The winter season of our lives is similar. Just as trees lose their leaves, our bodies begin to lose some of their abilities.

The winter of our life would be a sad season if all it contained were losses, but that doesn't need to be the case. "The winter which follows the autumn will not be barren if the harvest has been stored. For the woman who has accomplished the developmental tasks of the earlier periods, there will be a vital and meaningful winter season."[8] Proverbs 31:25 says that a woman who fears and reverences God will be a woman of strength and dignity, having no fear of old age. Women who have walked with God and lived full, rich lives discover winter to be a season of gain as well. Let's consider some of the losses and gains that take place during the winter season of our lives.

Dealing with the losses. My (Ellen's) in-laws are currently dealing with some of the losses of this season. My father-in-law, Frank, began losing some eyesight in his seventies as a result of macular degeneration. Because he loved to read and he liked the independence of driving, this was difficult. Now in his eighties, Frank has adapted well by listening to books and magazines on tape, available through the mail from the Library of Congress. He's thankful for people who have helped him with transportation.

My mother-in-law, Connie, began losing some of her height in her seventies. Although she once stood four or five inches taller than I, in her eighties she is an inch or two shorter. Recently I took some of Connie's pants and skirts to the tailor for alterations. Although she hadn't gained any weight (she's always been trim), the inches she had lost in height were being added around her waist, where the compacted inches of this season tend to settle. There just wasn't enough waistband to go around. She too has handled her losses with sweet acceptance. Frank and Connie have struck a healthy balance of dealing with their physical losses while acknowledging God's faithfulness.

Losses of sight, height, hearing and circulation are common, but never easy, for women in the winter season of life. Perhaps one of the biggest losses any woman in the winter of life experiences is the loss of her spouse. Doris, a friend who recently lost her husband, is dealing with the shock of his sudden death and grieving the loss of the close companionship they enjoyed. After her husband completed an illustrious career in the military, the two of them had grown especially close as they ministered together to the needs of people around them. Although she is feeling her loss keenly, she's noticing that serving others is helping her to heal.

The losses of this season bring with them an increased sense of vulnerability. Women in the winter season of life often need to depend more on people around them to help with tasks they can no longer accomplish on their own. The Bible graciously speaks to this vulnerability when it reminds us that from God's point of view one of our responsibilities as Christ-followers is to take care of our needy parents (Mark 7:5-13). Those of us who are caring for older people in this season can have the opportunity to ease—not exacerbate—their losses by treating them with love and respect. "Then listen to these old people in order to learn what life is, from the mouths of those who have lived it fully."[9]

Appreciating the gains. Thankfully, winter is also a season of gains. It's a time for remembering and recounting God's blessings in our life, a time for passing on blessings and traditions, and a time when we anticipate seeing the face of Jesus. Women who reflect on life with a sense of fulfillment and satisfaction are grateful, "gathering the experience of a long and eventful life into a meaningful pattern."[10] How precious to look back and reflect on God's *providence*—a word that is creeping into my (Joan's) vocabulary more and more. As we see how each season continues to build on the foundations established in the previous seasons, we realize that no experiences in our lives are wasted. Rather, we can be confident that God weaves together our cumulative experiences, accomplishing his purposes throughout our life.

The woman who has followed Christ through earlier seasons will no doubt have stories to tell the younger generations about God's faithfulness to her. In Joshua 3:6—4:9, after God holds back the waters of the Jordan River so that the children of Israel can carry the ark of God across the river on dry ground, Joshua instructs the people to build a monument using "stones of remembrance." Joshua tells the people that in the future, when their children ask, "What do these stones mean?" they can tell of God's provisions. We know of one family that keeps a basket of smooth, flat stones on the kitchen counter. With a permanent marker, they write on these stones answers to prayer and other examples of God's goodness, eager to remember and share with each other what he has done. We're wise to build stones of remembrance into our relationships, one at a time.

Another gain realized in the winter of a woman's life is the opportunity to pass down blessings and traditions from one generation to another. The Bible records many instances of one generation passing on a blessing to the next. Especially tender is the blessing given by Simeon to Jesus and his family. Simeon, a devout and righteous Jew, was promised by God's Spirit that he would not die until he had seen the long-awaited Messiah. When Mary and Joseph brought Jesus to the temple to present him to the Lord, Simeon recognized the child as the Messiah. He gathered the baby into his arms and said, "Lord, now I can die content! For I have seen him as you promised me I would. I have seen the Savior you have given to the world. He is the light that will shine upon the nations, and he will be the glory of your people Israel!" (Luke 2:29-31 LB). In the process of giving a blessing, Simeon also received a blessing, seeing the face of God's Anointed One before he died.

Maybe the blessings we pass down in the winter of our lives will not be recorded two thousand years later like Simeon's, but they can still have a lasting impact on the lives of the recipients. They may even become traditions—like the "white hanky" tradition in my (Joan's) family. Home movies from our China years captured my grandmother wiping tears from her eyes with a hanky as she waved goodbye to us. Since then, our family has used white hankies to carry on the tradition that Grandma started. When saying goodbye for any length of time, we often drive off with white hankies or flags flying from car windows and sunroofs. When our daughter Jill was married, white hankies were distributed to guests instead of rice or birdseed. Friends and family waved goodbye with the hankies as the bride and groom departed for their honeymoon. The long-standing hanky tradition became especially touching this year when my father died while sitting in his favorite chair, holding a white hanky in his hand. In light of our family's tradition, we

> *For to me, to live is Christ and to die is gain.*
> PHILIPPIANS 1:21

like to think that he was saying goodbye.

The most lasting gain in the winter of our lives, if we are Christ-followers, is that we will see the face of Jesus. As we become increasingly impressed with the brevity of our life on this planet, we long more and more for our eternal home. G. K. Chesterton referred to this as being homesick even while at home.

Erik Erikson labeled this last season of life as the stage of "integrity versus despair." How wonderful to be able to reflect on life with a sense of integrity and fulfillment. "I have fought the good fight, I have finished the race, I have kept the faith" (2 Timothy 4:7). How sad it would be to face the winter of life with a sense of despair, cynicism or regret for the life we had lived, and with dread and fear of death. We would have nothing to gain and everything to lose. But it need not be so! Any woman who still has the faculties and understanding to read this book also has an opportunity to end well, if she puts her hope in Christ.

Spring, summer, fall and winter—each season with its special joys and challenges yields to the next. It's comforting to know that the God who directs and sustains the seasons of the world also directs the seasons of our lives. Because

> *Jesus lives and so shall I;*
> *Death is but my*
> *entrance into glory.*
> *Courage then,*
> *my soul, for thou*
> *Hast a crown of life*
> *before thee.*
> *Thou shalt find thy*
> *hopes were just;*
> *Jesus is the*
> *Christian's trust.*
> CHRISTIAN F. GELLERT

he is the One who created us and understands us better than we understand ourselves, he is the One we depend on to sustain us, whether our seasons include balmy breezes or tropical hurricanes. As a result of exploring the seasons of our life, may we all become more intentional about how we're planting now, so that when harvest time comes we'll have plenty to go around!

Reflection Questions

1. What is your favorite season of the year? Why?

2. What is one challenge in your current season of life? What is one concern for a season yet to come?

3. How has it been helpful for you to gain an overview of seasons in a woman's life?

4. If you've attended any of your high school or college reunions, what have you observed about sowing and reaping?

5. Read Deuteronomy 30:19-20. What choices lead to life?

6. Read Joshua 3:6—4:9. What is one of your "stones of remembrance"?

7. How has a person in the wintertime of life blessed you?

Notes

Chapter 1: Why Does It Seem Like There's Not Enough of Me to Go Around?
[1]William Zinsser, *On Writing Well* (New York: HarperCollins, 1998), p. 84.

Chapter 2: I Can't Do It All, and I Can't Do Life Alone
[1]Francis Thompson, "The Hound of Heaven," in *Anthology of English Literature,* ed. M. H. Abrams (New York: W. W. Norton, 1979), p. 1732.
[2]Warren W. Wiersbe, *Bible Exposition Commentary* (Wheaton, Ill.: Victor, 1989), p. 127.
[3]Kathleen B. Nielson, *Resting Secure* (Grand Rapids, Mich.: Baker, 1993), p. 15.
[4]Robert C. Roberts, *The Strengths of a Christian* (Philadelphia: Westminster Press, 1984), p. 71.
[5]Douglas Rumford, *Soul Shaping* (Wheaton, Ill.: Tyndale House, 1996), p. 37.

Chapter 3: Confident Women Have More to Go Around
[1]Robert G. Barnes Jr., *Confident Kids* (Wheaton, Ill.: Tyndale House, 1987), p. 11.
[2]Ingrid Trobisch, *The Confident Woman* (New York: HarperCollins, 1993), p. 29.

Chapter 5: Help! We Need Boundaries!
[1]Henry Cloud, *Changes That Heal* (New York: HarperCollins, 1995), p. 162.
[2]Henry Cloud and John Townsend, *Boundaries in Marriage* (Grand Rapids, Mich.: Zondervan, 1999), p. 28.
[3]Ibid., p. 22.
[4]Patti Breitman and Connie Hatch, *How to Say No Without Feeling Guilty* (New York: Broadway, 2000), p. 152.
[5]Cloud, *Changes That Heal,* p. 150.
[6]Anne Katherine, *Boundaries* (New York: Parkside, 1991), p. 15.

Chapter 6: Families—Are They Making or Breaking Us?
[1]Dolores Curran, *Traits of a Healthy Family* (Minneapolis: Winston, 1983), p. 23.
[2]"Bagging Rites," *Chicago Tribune,* August 11, 1999, Sports, p. 1.
[3]Quoted in Ellen Banks Elwell, *The Christian Mom's Idea Book* (Wheaton, Ill.: Crossway, 1997), p. 130.
[4]Ingrid Trobisch, *The Confident Woman* (New York: HarperCollins, 1995), p. 32.
[5]John Townsend, *Hiding from Love* (Colorado Springs, Colo.: NavPress, 1991), p. 96.
[6]David Walls, *Learning to Love When Love Isn't Easy* (Wheaton, Ill.: Victor, 1992), p. 169.
[7]Michael E. McCullough, Steven J Sandage and Everett L. Worthington Jr., *To Forgive Is Human* (Downers Grove, Ill.: InterVarsity Press, 1997), p. 157.
[8]Judith Viorst, *Necessary Losses* (New York: Simon & Schuster, 1986), p. 175.
[9]D. W. Winnicott, *Home Is Where We Start From* (New York: Norton, 1986), p. 120.
[10]James Dobson, *Dare to Discipline* (Wheaton, Ill.: Tyndale House, 1970), p. 15.
[11]Gordon Allport, *The Individual and His Religion* (New York: Macmillan, 1953), p. 31.
[12]John Bowlby, *A Secure Base* (New York: BasicBooks, 1988), p. 11.
[13]Diana Baumrind, *Rearing Competent Children,* New Directions for Child Development (San Francisco: Jossey-Bass, 1989).
[14]Elwell, *Christian Mom's Idea Book,* p. 238.

Chapter 7: Fitting Friendships into a Busy Life
[1]Archibald Hart, *Me, Myself & I: How Far Should We Go in Our Search for Self-Fulfillment?* (Ann Arbor, Mich.: Servant, 1992), p. 202.
[2]David Livingstone, source unknown.
[3]Erich Fromm, *The Art of Loving* (New York: Harper & Row, 1956), p. 96.
[4]Mary Kay Shanley, "Circle of Friends," *Family Circle,* September 14, 1999, p. 140.
[5]Leland Ryken, James C. Wilhoit and Tremper Longman III, eds., *Dictionary of Biblical Imagery* (Downers Grove, Ill.: InterVarsity Press, 1998), p. 309.
[6]Ingrid Trobisch, *The Confident Woman* (New York: HarperCollins, 1993), p. 63.
[7]Gary Inrig, *Quality Friendship* (Chicago: Moody Press, 1981), p. 31.
[8]Dietrich Bonhoeffer, *Life Together* (New York: Harper & Row, 1954), p. 99.

Chapter 8: Hope When There Just Isn't Enough to Go Around
[1]Philip Yancey, *Disappointment with God* (Grand Rapids, Mich.: Zondervan, 1988), p. 36.
[2]Elisabeth Kübler-Ross, *On Death and Dying* (London: Macmillan, 1969).
[3]Amy Carmichael, *Toward Jerusalem* (London: Billing & Sons, 1936), p. 41.
[4]Susan Zonnebelt-Smenge and Robert DeVries, *Getting to the Other Side of Grief* (Grand Rapids, Mich.: Baker, 1998), p. 14.
[5]This story comes from James S. Hewett, ed., *Illustrations Unlimited* (Wheaton, Ill.: Tyndale House, 1988), pp. 292-93.
[6]R. T. Kendall, *God Meant It for Good* (Wheaton, Ill.: Tyndale House, 1988), p. 40.
[7]Peter Marshall, in James S. Hewett, ed., *Illustrations Unlimited* (Wheaton, Ill.: Tyndale House, 1988), pp. 139-40.
[8]C. S. Lewis, *The Problem of Pain* (New York: Macmillan, 1962), p. 93.
[9]James Dobson, *When God Doesn't Make Sense* (Wheaton, Ill.: Tyndale House, 1993), pp. 98-99.
[10]Donald McCullough, *The Trivialization of God* (Colorado Springs, Colo.: NavPress, 1995), p. 38.
[11]Paul Brand and Philip Yancey, *Fearfully and Wonderfully Made* (Grand Rapids, Mich.: Zondervan, 1980), p. 206.
[12]Joseph Bayly, *The Last Thing We Talk About* (Elgin, Ill.: David C. Cook, 1973), p. 105.
[13]Handley Moule, source unknown.

Chapter 9: Here and Now Is Just One Season of Life
[1]Paul Tournier, *The Seasons of Life* (Atlanta: John Knox Press, 1961), p. 61.
[2]Anita Spencer, *Seasons* (New York: Paulist, 1982), p. 20.
[3]Robert Bellah et al., *Habits of the Heart: Individualism and Commitment in American Life* (New York: Harper & Row, 1985), p. 57.
[4]Ruth and Dennis Gibson, *The Sandwich Years* (Grand Rapids, Mich.: Baker, 1991), p. 176.
[5]Daniel Offer and Melvin Sabshin, *Normality and the Life Cycle* (New York: BasicBooks, 1984), p. 167.
[6]Spencer, *Seasons,* p. 67.
[7]Judith Viorst, *Necessary Losses* (New York: Simon & Schuster, 1986), p. 230.
[8]Spencer, *Seasons,* p. 73.
[9]Paul Tournier, *Learn to Grow Old* (San Francisco: Harper & Row, 1972), p. 72.
[10]Erik Erikson et al., *Vital Development in Old Age* (New York: W. W. Norton, 1986), p. 288.